pathfinder® guide

2-44,

Edinburgh
and Lothians

WALKS

Compiled by
Brian Conduit and
John Brooks

D0278958

JARROLD

Acknowledgements
The publisher would like to thank Beverley Stirling at
Beecraigs Country Park and the Rangers at Almondell and
Calderwood Country Park for their advice.

Text:	Brian Conduit, John Brooks
Photography:	Brian Conduit, John Brooks
Editor:	Sarah Letts
Designers:	Doug Whitworth, Brian Skinner
Mapping:	Heather Pearson

Series Consultant: Brian Conduit

Jarrold Publishing   0-7117-1097-X

While every care has been taken to ensure the accuracy of
the route directions, the publishers cannot accept
responsibility for errors or omissions, or for changes in
details given. The countryside is not static: hedges and
fences can be removed, field boundaries can alter, footpaths
can be rerouted and changes in ownership can result in the
closure or diversion of some concessionary paths. Also, paths
that are easy and pleasant for walking in fine conditions may
become slippery, muddy and difficult in wet weather, while
stepping stones across rivers and streams may become
impassable.
   If you find an inaccuracy in either the text or the maps,
please write or email Jarrold Publishing at the addresses
below.

First published 2001
by Jarrold Publishing

Printed in Belgium
by Proost NV, Turnhout. 1/01

Jarrold Publishing,
Pathfinder Guides, Whitefriars, Norwich NR3 1TR
E-mail: pathfinder@jarrold.com

Front cover: View of Princes Street from Calton Hill,
         Edinburgh
Previous page: Edinburgh Castle

Contents

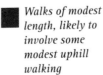

■ Short, easy walks

■ Walks of modest length, likely to involve some modest uphill walking

■ More challenging walks which may be longer and/or over more rugged terrain, often with some stiff climbs

TILLICOULTRY
DOLLAR
New Sauchie
Keilarsbrae
Coalsnaughton
Devonside
ALLOA
Clackmannan
Kennet
Dunmore
Airth
Kincardine Br
A876
Longannet Point
Power Station
CULROSS
GRANGEMOUTH
BO'NESS
FALKIRK
Redding
Polmont
Brightons
Maddiston
California
Standburn
Westfield
ARMADALE
Westrigg
WHITBURN
Harthill
Eastfield
Longridge
Stoneyburn
Fauldhouse
Greenburn
Addiewell
Breich
Forth
Braehead
West Mains
Yieldshields
Roadmeetings
Carstairs
West End
Carnwath
Newbigging
Walston
Dunsyre

King's Seat
Ben Cleuch
Castle Campbell
Pool of Muckhart
Yetts o' Muckhart
Rumbling Bridge
Crook of Devon
Tullibole Castle
Coldrain
Powmill
Blairingone
Cleish
Cleish Hills
Fort
Cult Hill
Hill End
Balgonar
Knock Hill
Saline
Cowstrandburn
Craigluscar Hill
Bowershall
Kingseat
Blairhall
Carnock
Gowkhall
Wellwood
Townhill
Oakley
Milesmark
Valleyfield
Carneyhill
Crossford
DUNFERMLINE
Low Torry
Torryburn
Abbey
Blair Abbey
Torry Bay
A985
Charlestown
Limekilns
Rosyth
St Margaret's Hope
North Queensferry
INVERKEITHING
Inverkeithing Bay
Forth Road Bridge
Forth Bridge
Dalmeny
QUEENSFERRY
Newton
Dundas Castle
Old Philpstoun
Philpstoun
Bridgend
Whitecross
LINLITHGOW
Linlithgow Bridge
Union Canal
Champany
The Binns
Blackness
Blackness Castle
Hopetoun House
Muirhouses
Carriden
Grangepans
Winchburgh
Broxburn
Kirkliston
Ratho Station
Edinburgh Airport
Ingliston
Gogar
A8
Cramond Bridge
Newbridge
Ecclesmachan
Uphall
Dechmont
Uphall Station
Burnside
Ratho
Bonnington
M8
LIVINGSTON
Deans
Livingston Village
Seafield
Dedridge
Oakbank
Kirknewton
Wilkieston
Currie
Balerno
BATHGATE
Boghall
Whiteside
East Whitburn
Blackburn
Polbeth
Bellsquarry
West Calder
Morton Resr
Threipmuir Resr
Harperrig Resr
Bavelaw Castle
Cobbinshaw Resr
Crosswood Resr
Woolfords Cottages
Tarbrax
Auchengray
Rootpark
Hare Hill
Springfield
Roman Fortlet
The Mount
Byrehope Mount
Baddinsgill Resr
Carlops
Bore Stane
North Esk Resr
Linton
Romannobridge
Black Mount
Dolphinton
Mountain Cross
Blyth

Loch Leven
St Serf's Island
Priory
Gairney Bank
Ballingry
Benarty Hill
Lochore
Glencraig
LOCHGELLY
KELTY
Loch Fitty
Hill of Beath
Crossgates
Fordell
Fordell Castle
Hillend
Dalgety Bay
Dalmeny
Cramond
M90
M9

SCALE 1:250 000 or 1 INCH to 4 MILES 1CM to 2.5KM

0 2 4 6 8 10 15 KILOMETRES
0 2 4 6 8 10 MILES

SCALE 1:250 000 or 1 INCH to 4 MILES *1CM to 2.5KM*

0 2 4 6 8 10 KILOMETRES 15

0 2 4 6 MILES 8 10

NBAR
Broxburn
Barns Ness
Skateraw
13
Power Station
Thorntonloch
Innerwick
Castle
Reed Point
Pease Bay
Siccar Point
Wheat Stack
1046
Cocklaw
Hill
Cockburnspath
Oldhamstocks
Fast Castle
Telegraph
Hill
ST ABB'S HEAD
Ecclaw
Fort
803
Meikle
Black Law
Lumsdaine
Cross Law
744
Forts
Northfield
St Abbs
909
Way
Blackburn
Rig
Grantshouse
Coldingham
Moor
12
Coldingham
Priory
Coldingham
Bay
Buss Craig
Heart
Law
1283
16
Southern
Upland
Houndwood
Ale
Water
Cairncross
B6438
EYEMOUTH
Cranshaws
Abbey
St Bathans
Ellemford
Broch
Fort
Fort
Fort
859
Horseley
Hill
Eye Water
Auchencrow
Reston
A1
Ayton
Castle
20
Burnmouth
Marygold
B6438
Lamberton
Beach
Longformacus
B6355
Lintlaw
Preston
B6437
712
Lamberton
15 Foulden
Clappers
Halidon
Hill
1333
Chimsidebridge
B6365
Edrom
Chirnside
Whiteadder
Water
A6105
307
ington
at Law
Castle
Hutton
Paxton
BERWICK-UPON-
DUNS
Allanton
B6460
B6461
Gavinton
165
Tweedmouth
East Ord
935
Polwarth
Blackadder
Fishwick
Tweed
Loanend
Longridge
Towers
355
Hule
Moss
A6105
Fogo
Whitsome
Horncliffe
Murton
Thornton
Aller
Dean
B6460
Horndean
Ladykirk
Cas
Norham
A698
Shoresdean
West
Allerdean
Ancroft
Greenlaw
Swinton
B6470
14
Grindon
Felkington
Swintonmill
Simprim
Shoreswood
B6354
Haydon
Dean
A697
Leitholm
356
Duddo
A6112
B6317
Bowsden
Hume
Lambden
Eccles
Lennel
225
Castle
Heaton
Etal
Barmoor
Castle
COLDSTREAM
Cornhill

Blackadder Water
Leet Water
MERSE

Walk	Page	Start	Nat. Grid Reference	Distance	Time
Arthur's Seat and Duddingston Loch	39	Holyrood Palace Edinburgh	NT767260	3½ miles (5.5km)	2hrs
Beecraigs and Cockleroy	36	Beecraigs Country Park	NT006747	4½ miles (7.2km)	3 hrs
Blackford Hill and the Hermitage of Braid	16	Car park on south side of Braid Hills	NT255700	2½ miles (4km)	1½ hrs
Caerketton and Allermuir Hills	58	Hillend Ski Centre Country Park	NT244668	4½ miles (7.2km)	2½ hrs
Clints Dod, Herring Road and Dunbar Common	84	Pressmennan Wood Car Park	NT621726	11 miles (17.7km)	5½ hrs
Dalkeith Demesne	29	Dalkeith Parish Church	NT334673	4½ miles (7.2km)	2 hrs
Dirleton and the Lothian Coast	34	Dirleton	NT514839	6 miles (9.5km)	3 hrs
Dunbar and John Muir Country Park	18	Dunbar	NT681792	3½ miles (5.5km)	2hrs
Edinburgh Old and New Towns	44	Scott Monument Princes Street	NT257739	5½ miles (8.9km)	2½ hrs
Gamelshiel Castle and Whiteadder Water	48	Whiteadder Reservoir	NT647643	4½ miles (7.2km)	2hrs
Haddington and the River Tyne	72	Haddington	NT514739	8½ miles (13.5km)	4½ hrs
Hailes Castle and Traprain Law	62	East Linton	NT592772	6½ miles (10.5km)	3½ hrs
Huntly Cot Hills and Hirendean Castle	65	Gladhouse Reservoir	NT309542	7½ miles (12km)	4½ hrs
Lammer Law and the Hopes Reservoir	87	Longyester	NT548657	8½ miles (13.7km)	4½ hrs
Linlithgow Loch	14	Linlithgow	NT000774	2½ miles (4km)	1½ hrs
Loganlea & Glencorse with Scald Law	68	Flotterstone Glen Countryside Info Service	NT309542	7½ miles (12km)	5 hrs
Monks Road and Cap Law	42	Nine Mile Burn	NT177577	4½ miles (7.2km)	2½ hrs
Monynut Edge	50	Upper Monynut Forest	NT694677	5½ miles (8.9km)	2½ hrs
North Berwick Law	32	Car park on west side of North Berwick Law	NT532841	3½ miles (5.5km)	2 hrs
Pencaitland and Ormiston	55	West Saltoun	NT454662	6½ miles (10.5km)	3 hrs
Pentland Ridge	80	Threipmuir Reservoir	NT167639	7½ miles (12km)	4½ hrs
Pressmennan Wood and Lake	22	Pressmennan Lake	NT629726	3 miles (4.8km)	2 hrs
Priestlaw Hill from Whiteadder Reservoir	60	Whiteadder Reservoir	NT644643	6 miles (9.7km)	3½ hrs
River Almond Walk	52	Mid Calder	NT078678	6½ miles (10.5km)	3½ hrs
Roslin Glen	24	Roslin Glen Country Park	NT273629	4 miles (6.5km)	2½ hrs
Shore Walk to Cramond	76	Hawes Inn South Queensferry	NT138784	8½ miles (13.5km)	4 hrs
Threipmuir and Harlaw Reservoirs	20	Threipmuir Reservoir	NT177639	3½ miles (5.6km)	2 hrs
Two Forth Bridges	26	The Binks South Queensferry	NT128787	4 miles (6.5km)	2½ hrs

Comments

The ascent of Arthur's Seat is quite exercising but is rewarded at the summit with breathtaking views of Edinburgh, the Lothian and Fife coasts and the Lammermuirs.

This is a popular venue for city dwellers at weekends but at other times the lake and surrounding woodland is left to the abundant wildlife. Cockleroy Hill provides a fine viewpoint.

This short but energetic walk takes in one of the great viewpoints for 'Auld Reekie'. Those using public transport can start the walk from Cluny Gardens on the opposite, north side, of the hill.

This Pentland walk is quite demanding involving a steep climb at the beginning, a section along a switchback ridge and a second ascent before the easy descent to the tranquil Swanston village.

The ascents and descents on this walk in the Lammermuirs are gentle and gradual but still afford magnificent views. The route may be difficult to follow in bad weather.

This walk takes in much of the great parkland surrounding Dalkeith House. There are also stretches which pass through farmland and shady woodland.

This walk begins in the charming village of Dirleton, continues across fields and then takes in a delightful stretch of sandy coastline with view across the Firth of Forth.

This impressive yet short and relaxing coastal walk begins in Dunbar, a popular seaside resort. Highlights of the route include Dunbar Castle, the 17th-century Town House and the Clifftop Trail.

This city walk explores the two sides of Edinburgh – the narrow streets and the closes of the Old Town and the contrasting broad thoroughfares and classical architecture north of Princes Street.

These hills are certainly lonely, and anyone enjoying solitude will find pleasure in this walk. After visiting the crumbling walls of the castle the way crosses the lower slopes of Spartleton.

Haddington lies at the centre of fertile agricultural land and is undoubtedly one of the most handsome villages in the Lothians. This walk follows the course of the River Tyne.

The distinctive Traprain Law provides the only steep (but short) climb on this interesting walk which includes features such as the River Tyne and the ruins of Hailes Castle.

The Moorfoots are the least known of the hills to the south of Edinburgh but they provide excellent walking, well illustrated here. There is a taxing climb to the ridge but it affords exhilarating views.

The combination of a challenging ascent and a walk in a secluded valley, by a burn, makes this route particularly rewarding.

The historic Linlithgow Palace and the church, one of the finest in Scotland, are always in view on this undemanding and delightful loch-side walk.

This is quite a demanding route with two steep ascents, the second one to reach the summit of Scald Law at 1898ft (579m). This route should not be attempted if visibility is poor.

There is a hard slog up to the Pentland Ridge where Scald Law is the main summit. The walking on top is excellent while the return by the two reservoirs is on a surfaced track.

This forest track runs above a burn and allows views of some beautiful scenery. The return over Heart Law demands good navigation and the route should not be attempted without a compass.

The climb comes right at the start of this route with the ascent of the Law, but the loss of breath is compensated by a wonderful view. The walk then takes in much of the historic and picturesque town.

Walkers using public transport can begin the walk from Ormiston or Pencaitland and perhaps divert to Glenkinichie distillery to make the day even more rewarding.

The peaks of West Kip, East Kip and Scald Law, on the Pentland range, are features on this demanding but exhilarating walk. This walk should not be attempted in bad weather.

The lakes and woods of this nature reserve hidden away on the northern slopes of the Lammermuirs are a haven for birds, mammals and insects. Pressmennan Wood is seldom disturbed by crowds.

This walk in secluded countryside begins at Whiteadder Reservoir and follows Faseny Water on the outward leg. The final section, the descent from Priestlaw Hill, requires care as it is over rough ground.

The Almondell Country Park is an oasis of beauty in Scotland's central industrial belt where the River Almond twists its way through a richly timbered gorge.

The ornately carved Roslin Chapel is the highlight of this route which initially passes through a thickly-wooded glen and later, on the return section, follows a track above it.

In summer the ferry should be operating (not on Friday's) so that public transport can be used to return to the city. If not, the route along the shore of the Firth is enjoyable in both directions.

There are no taxing gradients in this peaceful walk along the shores of two beautiful reservoirs. The Pentland hills provide dramatic backdrops and there are invariably a variety of species of waterfowl.

It might appear that walking 1½ miles across a bridge would make an unappealing walk but this is far from true in this case, with the railway bridge and busy waters of the Forth always in view.

Introduction to Edinburgh and Lothians

There can be few cities in Britain or indeed elsewhere that have a finer setting than Edinburgh. Its position on the southern shores of the Firth of Forth – at the eastern end of the central lowland belt between the Highlands to the north and the Southern Uplands to the south – made it the ideal site for Scotland's capital, even though it did not attain that role until the fifteenth century. The impressive landscape of the city was formed by geological action that occurred over millions of years ago, Arthur's Seat and Castle Rock were both part of the Edinburgh Volcano which erupted 325 million years ago, forming Calton Hill. About this remarkable landscape is built a beautiful and fascinating city, renowned throughout the world for its heritage and architecture. The area around Edinburgh, the Lothian region, has the same mix of coastal panoramas and dramatic vistas. From the Bass Rock and Berwick Law of North Berwick in East Lothian, through the Pentland Hills of Midlothian, to the historic royal burgh of Linlithgow in West Lothian, the region is rich in both terrain and heritage.

Superb mixture of hills and lowland

This is ideal country for walking: a superb mixture of empty rolling hills and expansive moorlands and delightful rivers, bounded by fertile lowlands and an impressive coastline.

Priestlaw Hill

Dalmeny Shore, South Queensferry

The hills begin almost in the centre of Edinburgh itself. When strolling down Princes Street, the impressive profile of Arthur's Seat dominates the skyline, rearing above Holyrood Park at the bottom end of the Royal Mile. The short, steep climb to its 823-ft (251-m) summit provides magnificent panoramic views over the city, across the Firth of Forth, along a lengthy stretch of the Lothian coast and across the flattish terrain to the south of Edinburgh to the outlines of the nearest hills.

Nearest of all are the Pentlands, whose smooth, steep slopes extend in a roller-coaster fashion south-westwards from the southern outskirts of the city. Despite a maximum height of only 1,898ft (579m), the abrupt manner in which they rise above the surrounding country gives them the appearance of a mountain range. With a large number of well-waymarked paths, they provide unrivalled walking opportunities right on the doorstep of the Scottish capital. The broken range of the Pentland Hills begins roughly 3 miles (4.8km) south west of Edinburgh and stretches some 16 miles (25.6km) into Lanarkshire. Views from the Pentland Ridge and particularly from the summit Scald Law are superb, taking in the Lammermuirs and the Firth of Forth.

Looking south-eastwards from the main Pentland ridge, the long lines of the Moorfoot and Lammermuir hills fill the horizon. The Lammermuirs are nearest the coast and create a broad wedge between the lowlands of East Lothian to the north and those of the Merse to the south. The Moorfoots present a steeper face and are more thickly forested, especially on their southern slopes, which descend to the Tweed valley.

The hills of the Scottish Borders are an obvious attraction for walkers, but the coast and the lowlands of East Lothian have plenty of attractions.

Duddingston Loch and village from Queen's Drive, Holyrood Park, Edinburgh

There are fine, bracing walks along the rugged cliffs of the Berwickshire coast; further north beyond Dunbar the coast becomes gentler, comprising a mixture of low cliffs, salt-marshes and dunes. The lowlands themselves are not flat but undulating, interspersed with low hills and punctuated with sharp, dramatic-looking volcanic outcrops: North Berwick Law, Traprain Law and the Bass Rock just off the coast, are all striking landmarks that can be seen for miles around. A delightful walk can be enjoyed in the valley of Whiteadder, while Lammer Law, one of the highest peaks of the Lammermuir Hills, provides a challenge. East Lothian has always been one of the most fertile and prosperous agricultural regions of Scotland and this can be seen on the walks that take in the red-tiled villages of East Lothian and the handsome and dignified buildings of Haddington.

West Lothian is a region with both agricultural and industrial heritage, though the coal mining that was once so prevalent in the small towns and villages has gone. Linlithgow in the north has a strong history as an ancient burgh and a remarkable palace that sits beside town's loch that makes a great attraction for visitors.

The walks in this book take advantage of variety in the terrain and landscape. The routes follow not only footpaths, but also a canal-side path, a disused railway line and even the Forth Road Bridge, while the walk in Edinburgh city centre enables the walker to contrast the hustle and bustle of the Old Town with the elegant ambience of the New Town.

Pressmennan Wood

Linlithgow Loch

Start	Linlithgow
Distance	2½ miles (4km)
Approximate time	1½ hours
Parking	Linlithgow
Refreshments	Pubs and cafés at Linlithgow
Ordnance Survey maps	Landranger 65 (Falkirk & West Lothian), Explorer 349 (Falkirk, Cumbernauld & Livingston)

The highlights of this flat and easy circuit around Linlithgow Loch are the constantly changing views of Linlithgow Palace and church perched above the southern shores. From the north-east corner the views across the loch are enhanced by the distinctive shape of Cockleroy in the background.

Two grand adjacent buildings dominate the old town of Linlithgow and all the views across the loch. The substantial ruins of Linlithgow Palace, popular residence of Stuart kings and birthplace of Mary Queen of Scots in 1542, date from the 15th to 17th centuries. Building was started by James I of

Scotland in 1425, and the work was completed around the middle of the 16th century. Extensions and repairs were carried out in the 17th century but the palace became a ruin when it was

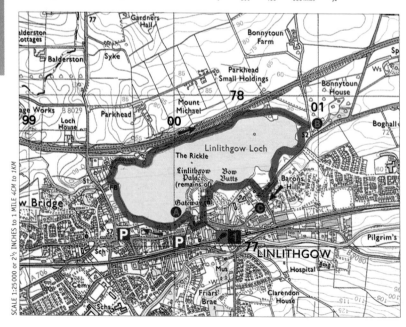

Linlithgow Palace from across the loch

carelessly set alight by some of the Duke of Cumberland's troops in 1746, following the Jacobite Rebellion. The church next to it, one of the finest in Scotland, dates from the 15th and 16th centuries, apart from the thin modern aluminium spire above the west tower.

The walk starts at Linlithgow Cross in the town centre. Facing the town hall, now the tourist information centre, turn left along The Vennel, shortly turn right at a sign 'Public Library and Public Toilet' and then turn left down to the lochside Ⓐ.

Follow a tarmac path beside a picnic and play area, which later curves to the right along the west side of the loch. All the way there are superb views of the palace and church above the loch from a variety of angles. In the north-west corner, cross a footbridge and turn right at a fork to continue along the north shore of the loch, passing some houses. After passing the last of the houses, the tarmac path becomes a rough path, screened from the nearby M9 by a grassy and wooded embankment on the left, but the noise of the traffic is inescapable. This is a particularly attractive stretch of the walk, at times passing between trees and gorse bushes and with superb views to the right of the palace with the prominent hill of Cockleroy beyond.

Just before emerging onto a lane, turn right Ⓑ through a kissing-gate to follow a grassy path beside the east shores of the loch, bending right to continue along the south shore. The path later bears left away from the loch, beside woodland on the right, to go through a kissing-gate onto a road. Turn right and then at a sign 'Linlithgow Peel and Palace' turn right again Ⓒ along a tarmac path between houses on the right and a church on the left, which heads downhill to rejoin the lochside.

Cross a footbridge and follow the tarmac path to the left to continue along the south side of the loch towards the palace and church. At a path junction below the palace ruins, turn left along an uphill path, later turning right to pass between the palace and church. Turn left through the palace gateway known as The Fore, built for James V around 1535 to give access to The Peel or outer enclosure of the palace, to return to the start. ●

Blackford Hill and the Hermitage of Braid

Blackford Hill and the Hermitage of Braid

Start	Car park on south side of Braid Hills Drive which runs between A701 and A702 on southern side of the city
Distance	2½ miles (4km)
Approximate time	1½ hours
Parking	At start
Refreshments	None on route
Ordnance Survey maps	Landranger 66 (Edinburgh, Penicuik & North Berwick), Explorer 350 (Edinburgh, Musselburgh & Queensferry)

Blackford Hill rises to a height of 539ft (164m) to overlook Edinburgh from the south. A beautiful wooded glen lies below the hill with a romantic Gothic house standing beside the burn at the centre. This is the Hermitage of Braid which serves as a visitor centre giving information about this popular nature reserve. There are several short but steep gradients.

Leave the car park, cross the busy road, and turn left. Walk for about 150 yards (137m) on the footpath before turning right through stone pillars and a kissing gate on to an enclosed footpath. This is the Lang Linn Path which descends to join another path in the trees at the top of the Hermitage of Braid woods Ⓐ.

Turn left and walk with railings on the left and a sheer drop to the right. A building will come into view below, partly hidden by the trees – this is the Hermitage. Continue on the top path but branch off it to the right on to one which descends steps to the burn at the bottom Ⓑ. Turn right on to an asphalt drive to reach the Hermitage of Braid Ⓒ – a Gothic villa in a fairytale setting. It was built in 1785 for Charles Gordon of Cluny.

Remain on the same side of the stream as the Hermitage and climb the steep path to the top of the woods. However, this is like a false summit as another climb follows, now with a wall to the left. At the top you are faced by a wall; turn right and walk for a few yards by the wall, go through an opening Ⓓ and turn left.

When the path divides take the right-hand fork which climbs the shoulder of the hill giving good views of Edinburgh Castle and the city skyline. The path dips down to a grassy space above Blackford Pond (an alternative place for starting this walk would be from the park entrance close to the pond). Cross the grass to climb a path on the far side. As you climb the Royal Observatory with its green dome comes into view on the left. Turn right to climb to the summit of Blackford Hill.

From the triangulation pillar head down towards the Observatory and pass

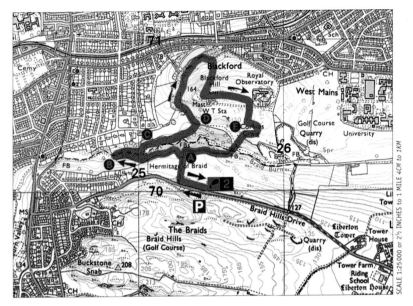

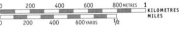

SCALE 1:25000 or 2½ INCHES to 1 MILE 4CM to 1KM

a small mast. From here you can see a grassy path leading south at the tail end of a rocky knoll. Make for this by turning right off the main path at a crossways, cross an asphalt track and then a grassy one. Turn left at the tail end of the crag **E** – the path soon drops down steeply. Bear right when it divides and turn sharp right to descend through a rocky gully. At the end of this fork left to drop down through trees to another path leading to a disused kissing gate. Take the steps down here to cross a high wooden bridge over the Braid Burn. On the other side there is a steep climb up steps with pointed railings on both sides. Turn left **A** when this enclosed path meets the Lang Linn Path used earlier and left again at the road to return to the car park.

0	200	400	600	800 METRES	1
					KILOMETRES MILES
0	200	400	600 YARDS	½	

The Hermitage of Braid

Dunbar and John Muir Country Park

Start	Dunbar
Distance	3½ miles (5.6km)
Approximate time	2 hours
Parking	Dunbar
Refreshments	Pubs and cafés at Dunbar
Ordnance Survey maps	Landranger 67 (Duns, Dunbar & Eyemouth), Explorer 351 (Dunbar & North Berwick, Musselburgh)

It is appropriate that the impressive stretch of coastline to the east of Dunbar, an area of cliffs, dunes and saltmarsh, should have been created a country park named after John Muir, for this native of Dunbar was one of the pioneers of the national parks movement in the USA. This short and relaxing walk explores part of the country park, following a well-waymarked trail along the cliffs from Dunbar Harbour to Belhaven Bay and returning to the town by way of a quiet road.

With fine sandy beaches and an attractive location, Dunbar has become a popular seaside resort but it is also a historic town. Of the once great castle – one of the most important medieval

fortresses in Scotland – only a few crumbling walls survive above the harbour, but the High Street contains the imposing 17th-century Town House and the birthplace of John Muir, now a museum. Muir was born in 1838, emigrated to America with his family at

Dunbar

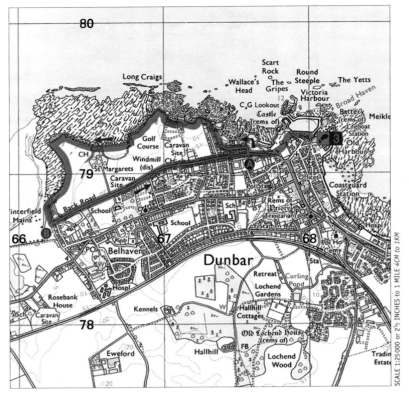

```
0    200    400    600    800 METRES   1
                                      KILOMETRES
                                      MILES
0    200    400    600 YARDS    ½
```

the age of eleven and later played a major role in the creation of the Yosemite and other national parks.

Begin the walk by the harbour and make your way to the fragmentary ruins of the castle at its west end. Just before reaching them, turn sharply left, almost doubling back, and then turn equally sharply right to walk along an uphill paved path. The path turns first left and then right to pass in front of Dunbar Leisure Pool at the start of a waymarked Clifftop Trail.

Continue along this paved path, which bears left to a road, turn right, turn right again 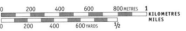 and after a few yards turn left along Bayswell Park. Where the road ends, bear right along a paved path, passing to the left of a war memorial. Now continue along a paved esplanade that twists and turns above the rocky coast, giving fine views to the right of Dunbar Castle and ahead to Bass Rock, Traprain Law, North Berwick Law and the wide, sandy expanse of Belhaven Bay. This Clifftop Trail is marked by a series of information boards. Turn left down steps, then down some more and turn right to continue along a path by the right-hand edge of a golf-course and above a stony beach.

The path follows the curve of Belhaven Bay sharply to the left, continuing above the bay and still alongside the edge of the golf course, later bearing right to reach the end of a lane by a group of wooden chalets. Follow the lane as it bends left to Shore Road car park and shortly afterwards take the first turning on the left ●.

The road heads steadily uphill, then levels off. Follow it for 1 mile (1.6km) back to Dunbar. ●

Threipmuir and Harlaw Reservoirs

Threipmuir and Harlaw Reservoirs

Start	Threipmuir Reservoir, south of Balerno
Distance	3½ miles (5.6km)
Approximate time	2 hours
Parking	Threipmuir car park on the left of the road running south from Balerno
Refreshments	None
Ordnance Survey maps	Landranger 65 (Falkirk & Linlithgow, Dunfermline), Explorer 344 (Pentland Hills, Penicuik & West Linton)

Besides being a lovely stroll along the shores of two man-made lakes, this walk also serves to give the newcomer an understanding of the geography of the Pentland Hills. Bird-lovers will find a variety of species both on the water and in the woodlands that fringe the reservoirs.

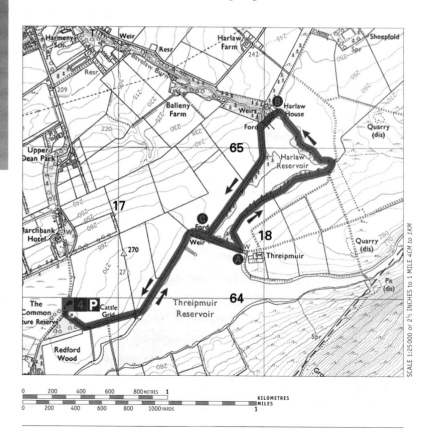

SCALE 1:25000 or 2½ INCHES to 1 MILE 4CM to 1KM

0   200   400   600   800 METRES   1
0   200   400   600   800   1000 YARDS

KILOMETRES
MILES
1

Harlaw Reservoir

From the car park go past the notice board and follow the track signposted to Harlaw. Keep ahead at the gate where the drive on the right goes to Easter Bavelaw, the farm on the other side of Threipmuir Reservoir. Once by the shoreline the track runs in a straight line relatively close to the water. There are sandy beaches by a rocky jetty at the northern end of the reservoir which are popular as paddling and bathing places. Turn right, cross the dam and then go through a kissing-gate on the left Ⓐ to walk by the side of Harlaw Reservoir.

This smaller reservoir has more trees around it though you have to be aware of cyclists who also use the narrow path, made rough by exposed tree roots. The scent of resin from the pine trees on a hot day is a memorable feature of the walk. The view north-eastwards to Allermuir Hill shows typical Pentlands scenery.

At Harlaw there is an information board about the natural and human history of the twin reservoirs. They were built between 1848 and 1890 in order to maintain a reliable supply of water for the Edinburgh water-powered mills which had previously relied solely on the Water of Leith. Turn left at the overflow channel Ⓑ to walk on a broad track along the western shore of Harlaw Reservoir which is also fringed with pine trees.

Rejoin the outward route at Threipmuir dam Ⓒ to return to the car park. The view of the Pentland Hills is stunning, with Scald Law and Black Hill easily identifiable. You may well spot a great crested grebe or a pair of teal on the water – both breed here though their favourite sites are at Bavelaw Marsh, at the very western end of the reservoir. ●

Pressmennan Wood and Lake

Start	The Woodland Trust car park at the west end of Pressmennan Lake, one mile south of Stenton. Note that there are no signposts to the wood in Stenton or on the lane from the village. See also Walk 27
Distance	3 miles (4.8km)
Approximate time	2 hours
Parking	At start
Refreshments	None
Ordnance Survey maps	Landranger 67 (Duns, Dunbar & Eyemouth area) Explorer 351 (Dunbar & North Berwick, Musselburgh)

The Woodland Trust own 210 acres of land on the south side of Pressmennan Lake, about four miles south-west of Dunbar. The narrow lake is man-made and the trees are mixed, deciduous predominating. The walk follows the shore of the lake on the outward section but returns on a higher path giving extensive views over East Lothian and beyond.

Pressmennan Wood

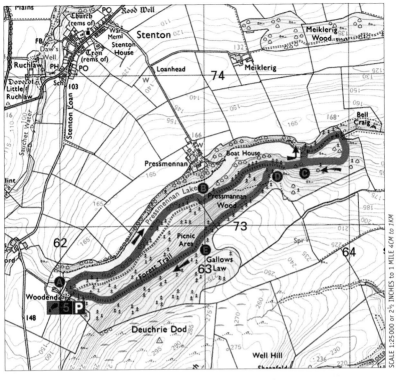

SCALE 1:25000 or 2½ INCHES to 1 MILE 4CM to 1KM

0 200 400 600 800 METRES 1
0 200 400 600 YARDS ½
KILOMETRES
MILES

Return to the entrance to the car park and find a path on the right which soon reaches a track. Turn sharply right again to take a path running beside a tiny burn. It soon reaches Pressmennan Lake Ⓐ, a narrow man-made stretch of water surrounded by magnificent trees. Note the wild raspberries which grow here. Nearby Stenton is noted for its soft fruit and birds have seeded the canes here. The twisting lakeside path, which must once have been choked by rhododendrons, reveals a succession of vistas. The path climbs to run by the edge of replanted woodland and then meanders amongst trees before climbing again to reach a memorial seat where it joins a track Ⓑ

Bear left along the track and pass a fallen beech tree which has been skillfully carved into a seat by use of a chainsaw. At the end of the lake Ⓒ steps take a path down to the dam. Walk across this and then take the grassy path away from the lake. This can be boggy in places.

Bear right before a gate leading into a field to follow the track which makes a sweeping right-hand turn and begins to climb. It proves to be the track left earlier for the dam. About 250 yards (229m) past the steps look for a path on the left Ⓓ which climbs through the trees giving ever more spectacular views northwards. These are at their best when the path reaches the top of the wood. North Berwick Law and Bass Rock are clearly visible. Wild flowers are abundant with honeysuckle climbing the trunks of many trees. Too soon the path reaches a wide grassy picnic area Ⓔ which provides a final chance of viewing the surrounding countryside. From here a track leads back through the trees to the car park. ●

Roslin Glen

Start	Roslin Glen Country Park
Distance	4 miles (6.4km)
Approximate time	2½ hours
Parking	Roslin Glen Country Park
Refreshments	Pub at Roslin
Ordnance Survey maps	Landranger 66 (Edinburgh & Midlothian), Explorer 344 (Pentland Hills, Penicuik & West Linton)

Below the village of Roslin the River North Esk flows through a dramatic, narrow, steep-sided and thickly wooded glen, part of which is now a country park. The first half of the walk follows an undulating path through the glen, and the return leg is along a track and lane above it, from which there are fine views of the long profile of the Pentland Hills. Near the end you pass the unusually ornate Roslin Chapel, well worth a visit.

Start by taking the path that runs parallel to the river, turning left to reach the riverbank at a footbridge. Cross the bridge over the North Esk, continue along an uphill path through woodland and, at the bottom of a flight of steps, turn right Ⓐ to pass under the bridge that leads to the sparse remains of the medieval Roslin Castle, largely destroyed by the English armies of Henry VIII in 1544, partially restored in the early 17th century and destroyed again by the English, this time under Cromwell, in 1650.

Descend via steps to a stone stile and footpath sign to Polton and turn left over the stile to start the walk through the thickly wooded glen. This is a superb walk through beautiful woodland, carpeted with bluebells in spring, and at times the cliffs on both sides of the glen are virtually perpendicular. After passing through a gap in a fence, you initially climb above the glen to reach a crossing of paths

near the top edge of the woodland. Turn right here along a path that descends steeply, zigzagging in places, to the bottom of the glen and turn left to continue by the river. Later the path heads quite steeply uphill to a stile. Climb it and continue along the top of the glen. There is a fine view through the trees on the right of the mainly 17th-century Hawthornden Castle on the other side of the gorge. After a while the path descends again to continue just above the river, with more open views to the left across fields.

Soon after climbing a stile, you emerge from the wooded glen and follow the river round a right-hand bend to another stile. Climb that and turn left away from the river to follow an uphill path between trees and gorse bushes to a crossing of paths Ⓑ. Turn left, head uphill through gorse onto a narrow ridge, between Roslin Glen to the left and Bilston Glen to the right, and continue steeply uphill along this narrow and crumbly ridge. At a fork, take the left-hand path and climb a stile onto a track on the edge of woodland.

Turn left along the track that keeps along the left edge of woodland, curving left. Later come fine views to the right of the Pentland Hills. Go through a metal gate and continue along a tarmac farm track – later a lane – into Roslin. Bear left to cross a bridge over a disused railway and continue through the village to a crossroads ●.

Turn left, and ahead is Roslin Chapel, which overlooks the glen. It was built in the 15th century by Henry Sinclair, Earl of Orkney, as a large collegiate church but only the choir was ever completed. The chapel is unusually flamboyant for a later medieval Scottish church, resembling contemporary churches in southern Spain or Portugal – and is particularly noted for its elaborate and intricate carvings.

Roslin Glen

Just before reaching the chapel, the route turns right, in the direction of the 'castle', downhill along a tarmac track. At a footpath sign for Polton, turn left along a walled track that bears right downhill back into the wooded glen. In front of a metal gate by the castle, head down a flight of steps to rejoin the outward route and retrace your steps to the start. ●

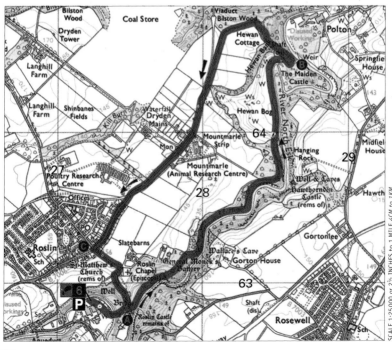

The Two Forth Bridges

The Two Forth Bridges

Start	The Binks, South Queensferry
Distance	4 miles (6.4km)
Approximate time	2½ hours (depending on train)
Parking	The Binks car park by the harbour, South Queensferry
Refreshments	Pubs and restaurants at South and North Queensferry
Ordnance Survey maps	Landranger 65 (Falkirk & Linlithgow, Dunfermline) Explorer 350 (Edinburgh, Musselburgh & Queensferry)

The frequent train service from North Queensferry to Dalmeny allows this wonderful scenic walk which involves crossing both bridges. The views from the pedestrian/cycle ways on the sides of the road bridge are spectacular though it should be noted that dogs are not permitted on the footways and that they are liable to be closed if conditions become too windy.

Queensferry is named after Margaret, second wife of King Malcolm Canmore, who died in 1093. This saintly lady was born in Hungary but arrived in Scotland as a refugee from the English court when her brother failed in his attempt to succeed to the English throne on the death of Edward the Confessor. Her marriage to Malcolm in 1070 proved to be exceptionally happy and Margaret became renowned for her piety and good works. One of the latter was the support she gave for a free ferry for pilgrims and the poor across the Forth – it sailed from the rocks here (The Binks), a natural landing-place.

Walk up from the car park and turn right opposite the police station. When you come to the bridge Ⓐ walk on the pavement beside the cycle track and when this divides fork left to take the walkway on the eastern side of the bridge, turning sharply to the right before the paybooths.

Even on this side of the bridge the view upriver is spectacular with the summit of Earl's Seat on the Campsie

Fells clearly visible. Ben Lomond can often be seen beyond. To the east the railway bridge predominates, its cantilever construction being as striking today as when it was opened in 1890. The three diamond-shaped sections used 55,000 tons of steel and 8 million rivets and cost the lives of 57 workmen.

The road bridge was completed in 1964 when it was the largest suspension bridge in Europe. Over a mile in length, its towers rise 512ft (156m) above the waters of the Forth and are set 1100 yards (1001m) apart.

On the northern side of the bridge descend the steps Ⓑ, cross the road, and turn left. Go through a kissing-gate to a path which leads to new housing. Turn left at the bottom and walk to a T-junction Ⓒ. Turn left again to climb a hill to rejoin the main road crossed earlier which brings you to North Queensferry, which in its heyday at the beginning of the 19th century

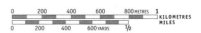

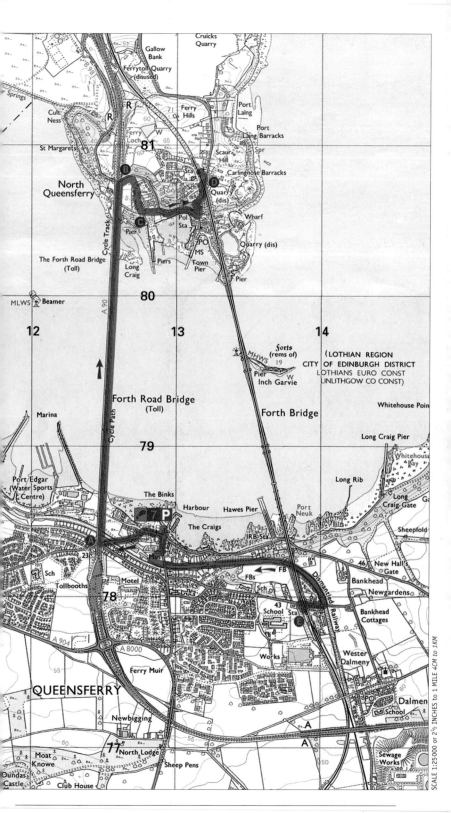

had 13 inns, catering for the innumerable ferrymen and their customers.

Turn left opposite Ferrybridge Inn to climb the steep hill (The Brae). Pass beneath a bridge and then join the Fife Coastal Path  to reach the railway station. Board a southbound train stopping at the next station, Dalmeny.

Turn right out of Dalmeny station to pass below the railway. After 200 yards (185m) there is another bridge crossing a disused railway line. Cross the bridge, descend steps on the right, and turn right at the bottom. Walk through a shady cutting which goes underneath the railway line approaching the Forth Bridge. Later the former railway track runs on a terrace above South Queensferry, and though in summer trees screen the view for much of the way there is a good viewpoint just after a footbridge. Note the famous Hawes Inn standing at the bridge end of the waterfront which was made famous by Robert Louis Stevenson in *Kidnapped*.

The old railway trackbed ends at the supermarket car park just above The Binks. Leave this and turn left to descend to the starting point.

The two Forth Bridges

Dalkeith Demesne

Start	Dalkeith Parish church (St Nicholas') in the High Street
Distance	4½ miles (7.25km)
Approximate time	2 hours
Parking	Roadside parking near start or at Dalkeith Country Park
Refreshments	Pubs and restaurants in Dalkeith. café at stables, Dalkeith Country Park
Ordnance Survey maps	Landranger 66 (Edinburgh, Penicuik & North Berwick) Explorer 350 (Edinburgh, Musselburgh & Queensferry)

This shortish walk through the grounds of Dalkeith Country Park may best be regarded as a family walk as children will find great fun in the elaborate adventure playground there. Because of this and the other facilities offered in the Country Park, Buccleuch Estates make a charge for entry between 10am and 6pm in the summer. In winter there is usually shooting on the estate on Wednesdays.

St Nicholas' parish church in Dalkeith High Street dates from the 13th century but has undergone a series of alterations over subsequent ages which have favoured some parts but left others ruinous. A menacing gargoyle overlooks equally sinister gravestones in the churchyard. From the church, walk eastwards down the broad High Street and keep ahead when the main road turns right. Go through the gates of Dalkeith Country Park Ⓐ.

Keep straight on down the drive to pass the extensive adventure playground and come to the magnificent stableyard built by William Adam *c.*1740 which now houses the Ranger's office as well as a café, toilets and shop.

The route skirts the back of the stables to pass to the left of the beautiful (but roofless) conservatory which was the work of William Burn,

1832-4. On the left is the Laundry House which gives its name to the bridge across the River South Esk which is crossed here.

Walk along a straight track which crosses farmland and gives views over pleasant countryside. After passing beneath electricity cables the track divides. Take the left fork and turn left before the farm to descend to Smeaton Bridge. Cross this and walk up the track for about 100 yards (91m) before turning sharply left Ⓑ on to a track obviously frequently used by horses. This gives pleasant walking high above the river and you pass beneath the electricity cables again. Just beyond this point there is a crossways Ⓒ where it is interesting to divert off the route (which continues ahead) by turning left to descend to a wooden footbridge over the river. This is the Meeting of the Waters where the South and North

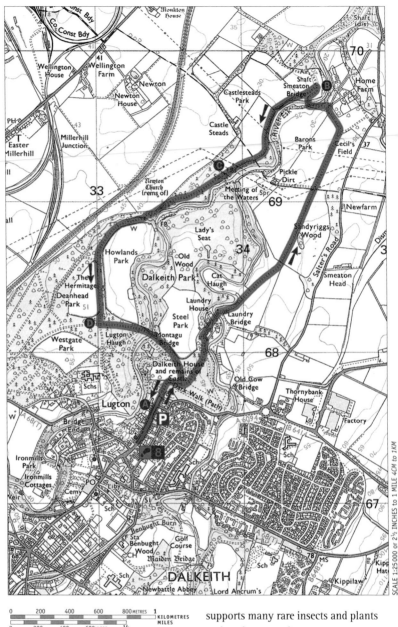

0	200	400	600	800 METRES	1

KILOMETRES
MILES

0	200	400	600 YARDS	1/2

SCALE 1:25000 or 2½ INCHES to 1 MILE 4CM to 1KM

Rivers Esk join. The woodland here is part of The Old Wood, an oak wood where most of the trees are 300 years old though their forebears date from the time when the Caledonian Forest flourished. It is a Site of Special Scientific Interest where the habitat supports many rare insects and plants and so the estate does not encourage access.

Return to the main track and continue along it. Traffic noise steadily increases from the City Bypass which forms the north eastern boundary of the park. Keep ahead when a track joins from the right and remain on the main track when another leaves to the right.

A climb follows after a bridge and you pass a well called the Marble Basin, restored in 1994. The trees here were planted in 1943. The track bends to the left at a tree nursery and having passed this it meets a broad driveway. Turn left here  and cross Montagu Bridge, the work of Robert Adam in 1792. Two life-sized statues of stags originally stood on its parapets but they so frightened horses that they had to be removed. Do not follow the drive to the right which leads to the House, now the Scottish Campus of the Universities of Wisconsin, but continue ahead and pass a picnic area. After this there is a second driveway joining from the right. Go through the small gate on the right at this junction and walk across the meadow facing the house.

Dalkeith House incorporates some of the fabric of the 12th century Dalkeith Castle but there is no sign of this from the outside. What we see is a palatial mansion dating from the last years of the 17th century, the work of James Smith who was commissioned by the first Duchess of Buccleuch. Subsequently both Vanbrugh and Robert Adam extended and altered the building.

Bear right on the far side of the meadow (or left to visit the adventure playground or café) and then leave the estate through the main gates and continue ahead to return to the starting point. ●

Dalkeith House

North Berwick Law

Start	Car park on west side of hill off B1347
Distance	3½ miles (5.6km)
Approximate time	2 hours
Parking	At start
Refreshments	Pubs and restaurants in North Berwick
Ordnance Survey maps	Landrangers 66 (Edinburgh, Penicuik & North Berwick) and 67 (Duns, Dunbar & Eyemouth area), Explorer 351 (Dunbar, North Berwick & Musselburgh)

The Law can be seen as a landmark from many of the other summits featured in this book and is, like Arthur's Seat and Bass Rock, the core of an ancient volcano. It is the finest viewpoint of the East Lothian coast and a clear day is essential for the climb. The rest of the walk may seem an anti-climax, but there is plenty of interest in the buildings of the town while the shady Glen contrasts well with the open countryside seen earlier.

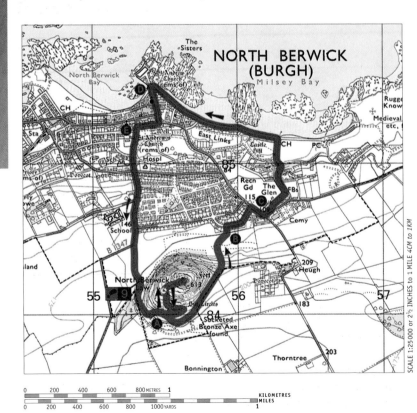

SCALE 1:25000 or 2½ INCHES to 1 MILE 4CM to 1KM

The Law suffers from fragile soil so it is as well to obey the advice given on the plaque at the start to stay on the waymarked paths (though these may be hard to spot in places). The path initially skirts a wood as it swings around the south side of the Law beneath low cliffs. The letters 'GBH' are painted in white at the end of these and having passed this point  the clearly-defined grassy path becomes very steep for a short distance. Then it bends right to make a more gradual ascent. Tantallon Castle comes into view ahead and then the path begins to zigzag. Within half an hour of leaving the car park you should be at the top of the

North Berwick Law

Law where there is an ancient whalebone, a triangulation pillar, and a viewpoint indicator.

Retrace your steps from the summit until you catch sight of the pond on the western side of the Law. You will first pass a white bench and then a white seat. The path gradually swings northwards and the tower of a disused windmill lies ahead. You may see wild goats grazing on the hillside amongst the sheep.

At the bottom of the Law 🅐 bear left on a sheep track just above the fence. This gradually swings round to give views towards the town. Looking in this direction you will see a gate in a wall in the front of houses. Make for this 🅑 by zigzagging down to the lower ground taking care to skirt the dense whin and avoid boggy patches.

Go through the kissing gate and turn right at the road. Pass the entrance to a supermarket and turn right at the main road. Cross the road to take a path 🅒 waymarked to 'The Glen'. This follows a small burn with a playing field to the left at first. Then it plunges into more dense woodland and continues to follow the course of the burn, emerging into the open by a golf clubhouse. Turn left at the shore and follow the road round to the harbour. Turn sharp left at the Lifeboat Station 🅓 towards the Law to pass the Baptist chapel and go down Quality Street to the Tourist Information Centre. Pass this and bear right at Kirk Pots passing the romantic ruins of St Andrew's Church. Beyond this turn left following the sign to North Berwick Law 🅔. Climb the hill and pass the Sports Centre and School to keep ahead when the main road sweeps right and thus reach the car park. ●

Dirleton and the Lothian coast

Start	Dirleton
Distance	6 miles (9.5km)
Approximate time	3 hours
Parking	Dirleton
Refreshments	Pub and tearooms at Dirleton
Ordnance Survey maps	Landranger 66 (Edinburgh & Midlothian), Explorer 351 (Dunbar, North Berwick & Musselburgh)

This flat walk starts in an outstandingly attractive village with a medieval castle and continues by way of tracks and field paths to reach the coast at Yellow Craig. It then follows a delightful ramble across dunes and along the edge of sandy beaches with fine views across the Firth of Forth to the Fife coast. For much of the way two well-known landmarks dominate the skyline: Bass Rock and North Berwick Law.

Dirleton must rank as one of the most attractive villages in Scotland, with 18th- and 19th-century cottages grouped around a spacious green that lies between the medieval castle and 17th-century church. The castle is not only a fine and well-preserved building itself but is enhanced by its surroundings of yew trees, a 17th-century bowling-green and colourful and well-tended flower borders. It became a ruin after its capture by General George Monk, 1st Duke of Albemarle, in 1650, during Cromwell's invasion of Scotland.

Begin by heading across to the church, pass to the right of it and walk along the straight, partially hedge-lined track. Where the track bends right, keep ahead along a grassy track between fields. To the right are fine views of both North Berwick Law and Bass Rock. On the far side, bear right to continue along the

Dirleton Castle

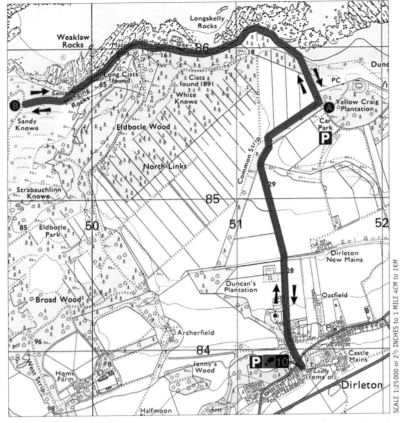

left-hand edge of a field, by a wire fence bordering woodland on the left, and turn left to climb a stile in that fence.

Continue through a narrow belt of trees to go through a gate and turn right along the right-hand edge of a field, now by a wire fence bordering woodland on the right. In the field corner go through a fence gap, turn right along a sandy path to a crossing of paths, keep ahead for a few yards and then turn left Ⓐ along a track to the coast.

On reaching the sea, turn left and, keeping to the right of scrub and trees all the while, follow a sandy path across the dunes or, where the path disappears at times, walk along the edge of the beach. This is a most attractive stretch of coast with fine views across rocks and sand of the Firth of Forth and with the hills of Fife on the horizon. You can turn back at any time, but for the full walk continue to where the coast bears left and pass to the right of a large house, before descending to walk along the beach below cliffs. A concrete post marks where a path bears left uphill over the dunes and across the neck of the headland to where there is a fine view at the top over Gullane Bay Ⓑ.

From here retrace your steps back to Dirleton. On this return leg there are particularly good views of both Bass Rock and North Berwick Law and, on approaching Dirleton, a superb view across the fields to the castle with the line of the Lammermuir Hills beyond. ●

Beecraigs and Cockleroy

Start	Park Centre, Beecraigs Country Park 3 miles south of Linlithgow
Distance	4½ miles (7.2km)
Approximate time	3 hours
Parking	Car park at start
Refreshments	Restaurant opposite Park Centre. Light refreshments at Park Centre
Ordnance Survey maps	Landranger 65 (Falkirk & Linlithgow, Dunfermline), Explorer 349 (Falkirk, Cumbernauld & Livingston)

Beecraigs Country Park crams a diverse range of activities into its 913 acres. Human occupations cover a wide range of open-air pursuits from archery to orienteering, and there is also room for commercial deer and fish farms. The route goes through the mature woodlands of the park to Cockleroy Hill, which though of modest height of 912ft (278m) is one of the finest viewpoints of lowland Scotland.

From the car park go through the gate (or over the bridge) into the deer farm. There is a distant view of the Forth bridges. Pigs are kept in enclosures here as well as deer which seem indifferent to visitors, even inquisitive children. The path enters woodland. At Beecraigs Loch turn left ⓐ to follow the shoreline in a clockwise direction. The tree-edged loch is well-stocked and very popular with anglers. An interpretation board is situated by a badger sett which has been in existence here for many years. Bear right following a red waymark to walk along the dam wall before going down the steps opposite the trout farm. This is used as an educational resource and the brown and rainbow trout reared here are put into Beecraigs and other nearby waters when old enough. Climb the track away from the fish farm to pass the anglers' lodge and continue around the perimeter of the loch.

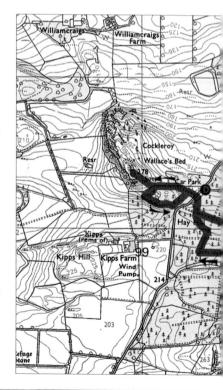

Opposite the island, and just after crossing a bridge, turn left following the red waymark. Cross the burn and climb into the wood. There is a road to the right which the path soon crosses 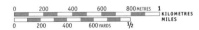 to a signpost pointing to Balvormie. The path winds through trees to a crossways – turn left to stay on the red route. However at the next waymark abandon the red route. Do not cross the bridge but keep ahead to cross another bridge a little way downstream. There are dense trees to the right and a wall to the left. Cross over a forest track to another on the other side and keep ahead following the wall when this becomes a path used by ponies. At the road turn right and cross it to a metal gate with a gap on the left. Go through this to walk on a track with Balvormie Meadow on the right.

Turn right at a T-junction following a fingerpost pointing to Balvormie and then bear left on a track into the forest.

Turn right at the next T-junction to arrive at a small circular clearing. Cross this to a path opposite which goes over a plank causeway and then climbs to meet another path. At the top turn sharp left and then right on to a short muddy track leading to another T-junction. Turn right here and then, after 20 yards, left on a path descending through trees to a plank causeway. After this climb a slight gradient and bear left to reach the road .

Cross the road and keep ahead by the car park on a forest track which climbs beside a wall. Climb the stile on the right and the grassy slope to the summit of Cockleroy Hill (912ft/278m) with its triangulation pillar and indicator. The view extends from Bass Rock in the east to Goat Fell on the Isle of Arran to the west. Ben Vorlich and Ben More are two

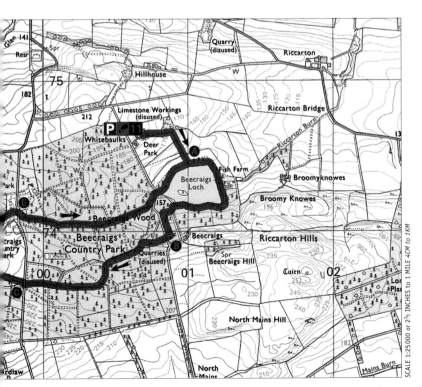

of the Trossach summits which can be identified.

Return to the stile and keep ahead on the blue waymarked route to return to the road, Cross the road ⓓ and bear right to retrace steps over the causeway following blue waymarks. Keep ahead to pass toilets and come to the picnic area and pond ⓔ. Go across the road and through the car park to find the red and dark blue waymarks at the southern end.

A broad, well-surfaced path descends gently. Keep ahead on the red path when the blue branches to the right. A gate faces you when you reach the road. Turn left before the gate and cross a footbridge to reach the Lochside car park. Cross the road here and follow the red waymarks around the west shore of the loch crossing a plank causeway. Continue walking through the trees and at a second causeway (which has a wheelchair ramp) turn left to return on the path through the deer farm to the Park Centre. ●

The stunning view from Cockleroy Hill

Arthur's Seat and Duddingston Loch

Start	Palace of Holyroodhouse, Edinburgh
Distance	3½ miles (5.5km)
Approximate time	2 hours
Parking	Car park just beyond entrance to palace
Refreshments	None on the way but plenty in Edinburgh
Ordnance Survey maps	Landranger 66 (Edinburgh & Midlothian), Explorer 350 (Edinburgh, Musselburgh & Queensferry)

There is a ruggedness and sense of remoteness on parts of this walk in Holyrood Park that makes it difficult to believe that you are within the city boundaries of Edinburgh, scarcely a stone's throw from the bustle of Princes Street. Despite its modest height of 823ft (251m), the climb up to Arthur's Seat is quite steep and exhausting but the view from the top surpasses that of many higher peaks, stretching right across Lowland Scotland and along the Lothian coast. After descending, the route continues by way of the village of Duddingston and beside Duddingston Loch. The final section over Salisbury Crags gives particularly dramatic views of the irregular jumble of buildings and spires that create the picturesque skyline of Scotland's capital.

The Palace of Holyroodhouse at the bottom end of Edinburgh's Royal Mile began life as the guest house of Holyrood Abbey, substantial portions of which survive on its north side. It was begun by James IV in 1501, but most of the present building dates from the late 17th century when it was rebuilt by Charles II following destruction. Holyrood Park was originally the park attached to the palace. With the steep, rocky, volcanic slopes of Arthur's Seat and the three lochs around its base, it gives the impression that a piece of the Highlands has been transported to the suburbs of Edinburgh.

Begin by crossing the road from the car park into the park and turning left along a gently ascending tarmac track. St Margaret's Loch is soon seen ahead. The track curves right. At a fork, take the left-hand path that descends slightly into the flat, grassy valley known as Dry Dam or Long Row. On the hill ahead are the scanty ruins of St Antony's Chapel, overlooking the loch.

Bear right Ⓐ along a clear, grassy path for the ascent of Arthur's Seat. At first the path climbs steadily through the valley, making directly for the blunt, prominent bulk of Arthur's Seat; later the going becomes steeper. Follow the path as it veers left, climbs a series

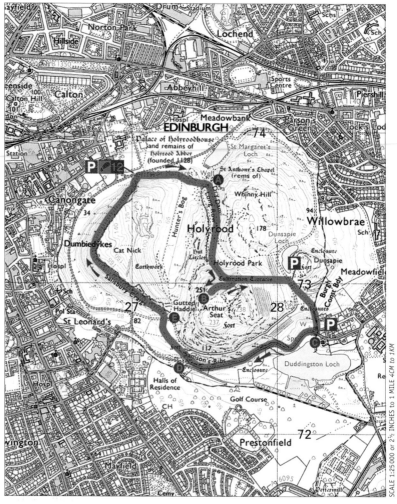

of steps and continues more gently upwards across the face of the hill, before bending sharply to the right to begin the final leg to the summit, marked by a triangulation pillar and view indicator . The all-round views are magnificent, taking in the Lothian coast with Bass Rock, the Lammermuir and Pentland hills, the Firth of Forth, the Fife coast and the Old Town of Edinburgh, the latter dominated inevitably by the castle.

Start the descent by retracing your steps to where the path bends sharply to the left. Here leave the outward route by keeping ahead in the direction of

Dunsapie Loch below, descending easily along a broad, smooth, grassy path to reach the road that encircles the park, opposite a car park and just to the right of the loch. Cross the road and, in the right-hand corner of the car park, turn right along a path that skirts the base of the hill on the left. At a fork, take the right-hand path downhill towards a wall, turn right alongside the wall and descend a long flight of steps to a road ⓒ. If you wish to visit Duddingston village – a rural enclave with a 12th-century church perched above the loch – turn left. Otherwise, turn right along the winding road above Duddingston Loch on the left and later below the almost perpendicular, rocky, gorse-covered slopes of Samson's Ribs on the right.

Bear right off the road  along a grassy path to follow the base of the slopes as they bear right, heading gently uphill towards the prominent jagged outlines of Salisbury Crags, to reach the park circular road again. Turn right for a few yards and, where the road bends right, turn sharp left  onto a stony track that heads steadily uphill, flattens out and then descends quite steeply across the face of Salisbury Crags. This is the Radical Road, constructed in the 1820s allegedly to provide work for the unemployed, and from it there are superb views to the left across Edinburgh.

The track reaches the circular road opposite the car park and starting point of the walk.

Dunsapie Loch

Monks Road and Cap Law

Start	Nine Mile Burn
Distance	4½ miles (7.25km)
Approximate time	2½ hours
Parking	Nine Mile Burn
Refreshments	None
Ordnance Survey maps	Landranger 65 (Falkirk & West Lothian), Explorer 344 (Pentland Hills, Penicuik & West Linton)

This fine, fresh, open walk on the eastern slopes of the Pentland Hills ascends Cap Law by way of the Monks Road, an ancient and well-defined path, to reach the base of the main Pentland ridge below West Kip. On the almost parallel descent, there are superb views ahead across the lowlands of the North Esk and South Esk rivers to the distant line of the Moorfoots and Lammermuirs. Route-finding could be difficult in bad weather and misty conditions.

In the corner of the car park at Nine Mile Burn, go through a gate at a public footpath sign for Balerno via Braid Law and walk along the enclosed track ahead. This is part of a Roman road. At a right-of-way sign in front of a gate, turn left and head uphill along the right-hand edge of a field, by a wall on the right, to climb a stone stile in the top corner **Ⓐ**.

Turn left alongside the wall on the left and, a few yards after passing a stile on the left, turn right **Ⓑ** at the end of a clump of gorse onto a faint but discernible path that heads gently uphill across grass, parallel to a narrow valley on the left and making for the rounded peak ahead. Climb a stile in a wire fence just in front of a wall, go through a gap in the wall and continue walking steadily uphill along the clear path ahead, the Monks Road, over Scroggy Hill, Monks Rig and Cap Law. There are grand views ahead across smooth, grassy slopes of the main ridge of the Pentlands. The path heads towards the base of the prominent peak of West Kip and eventually

A view of the Lammermuir and Moorfoot hills from the Pentlands

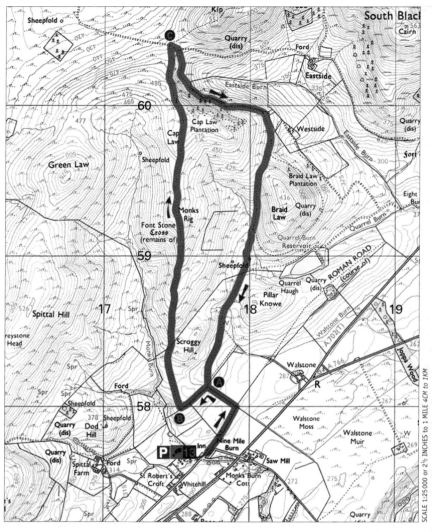

descends to a stile. Climb this stile and turn right along a track just below West Kip .

After about 100 yards (91m), turn right over the next stile, at a public footpath sign for Nine Mile Burn, along a path that bears left and contours the side of the hill, passing below a small plantation. Follow the path gently downhill, bear right on joining another path, by another public footpath sign for Nine Mile Burn, head over the shoulder of a hill and then continue gently downhill below the slopes of Braid Law on the left. Ahead there are magnificent views across the lowlands

to the line of the Moorfoot Hills, and on the right is the ridge traversed on the outward route.

Climb first a stile in a wire fence, then a stone stile in the wall directly ahead and bear right to continue along a clear path across grassland and bracken, eventually heading slightly uphill to a wire fence and beyond it to a wall and stone stile ●. Climb the stile, here rejoining the outward route, and retrace your steps to the starting point of the walk. ●

Edinburgh Old and New Towns

Edinburgh Old and New Towns

Start	Scott Monument, Princes Street, Edinburgh
Distance	5½ miles (8.9km)
Approximate time	2½ hours
Parking	Wide choice of city centre car parks – street parking free on Sundays
Refreshments	Many pubs and restaurants passed en route
Ordnance Survey maps	Landranger 66 (Edinburgh, Penicuik & North Berwick), Explorer 350 (Edinburgh, Musselburgh & Queensferry)

This city centre walk gives the visitor the opportunity to compare the contrasting architecture of the Old Town (16th and 17th centuries) with that of the New Town (18th and 19th centuries). It also climbs to the summit of Calton Hill and descends to walk by the refreshing Water of Leith through Dean Village.

Walk westwards down Princes Street (with the castle on the left) and pass Hanover Street, Frederick Street and Castle Street, three of the major south-north thoroughfares of the New Town. The plan for the latter was drawn up in 1767 and entailed the draining of a loch and the construction of a new bridge (North Bridge) to link the new part of the city with the old. Within an area of about one square mile a grid of streets was laid out and more than 11,000 houses built on them, transforming a wasteland of boggy ground into a new town with buildings to rival those of London or Bath. Princes Street is probably as famous as any street in Britain but from its beginning in 1769 has never been as elegant as the other streets of the New Town. At its completion in 1805 nearly all of the premises were already devoted to commerce, and development in the 20th century has given it the sort of

buildings that may be seen in any shopping centre throughout Britain.

At the western end of Princes Street turn right into South Charlotte Street ● which leads to Charlotte Square. Here the architecture is the finest the New Town has to offer with palatial houses for the nobility designed by Robert Adam in 1791. Both the north and south sides of the square have imposing classical façades which conceal eleven separate and individual three-storey houses. The National Trust for Scotland owns the Georgian House on the north side where visitors can get an impression of how life was lived by the wealthy and their servants in late 18th-century Edinburgh.

Having walked down the eastern side of Charlotte Square cross St Colme Street into Forres Street to reach Moray Place, which nameplates show to be a favourite address for Scottish institutions. Turn right into Darnaway

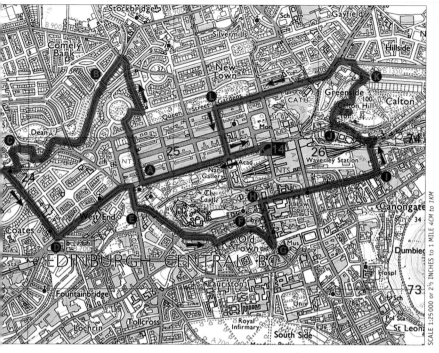

SCALE 1:25000 or 2½ INCHES to 1 MILE 4CM to 1KM

0	200	400	600	800 METRES	1
					KILOMETRES
					MILES
0	200	400	600 YARDS		½

Street and then left down Gloucester Lane, a mews where the courtyards would once have bustled with grooms getting horses and carriages ready for their masters. The rear aspects of the Georgian houses fronting India Street and Gloucester Street are also interesting. Just beyond Gloucester Place is one of the few pre-Georgian houses to survive in the New Town. Built in 1605 and with the motto 'For God Only', in 1798 it was the birthplace of David Roberts, the celebrated landscape artist.

Turn left into Grenville Place and then left again to walk down Saunders Street following a sign to St Bernard's Well and Dean Village. Go through what looks like a tunnel ● at the end of the street on to the start of the path which runs southwards along the east bank of the Water of Leith. The Doric temple on the right, with its statue of Hygieia, Goddess of Health, is the wellhouse of St Bernard's Well whose waters (which are sulphurous and reputedly have a repellent taste) were

nonetheless once thought beneficial.

Pass below Dean Bridge, designed by Telford and built 1829–32, to reach Dean village which was the hub of Edinburgh's medieval prosperity having 11 grain mills powered by watermills. The three millstones by the information board to the right are a reminder of the industry as is the cobbled street named Miller Row which leads to a bridge. Do not miss the picturesque house standing by the bridge but then cross it and turn left down Damside. At the second main opening turn left again and cross a footbridge ● which gives a wonderful view of Dean Village, ancient and modern.

Climb Hawthornbank Lane to Belford Road and bear right to reach Douglas Gardens. Turn left by the church and continue down Palmerston Place to St Mary's Episcopal Cathedral. The picturesque house just before the cathedral dates from 1617 and was the home of the Misses Walker whose legacy financed the building of the cathedral in 1870. The architect was Sir George Gilbert Scott and it is considered to be one of the finest of his designs, executed in typically florid Gothic style.

Turn left at the end of Palmerston Place  to reach Shandwick Place and walk to the end. Cross at the traffic lights to turn right into Lothian Road  and then take the first turning left into King's Stables Road which leads to the Grassmarket.

Walk to the east end of Grassmarket (scene of many executions in Covenanting times) and bear right into Candlemaker Row  – the tall houses here are typical of the Old Town. Greyfriars kirkyard is to the right where the array of monuments is unmatched in Scotland and shed light on many aspects of the nation's history. At the top of the Row is the famous effigy of Greyfriars' Bobby, a policeman's Skye terrier who, on the death of his master, carried on patrolling the Grassmarket for several years until he died in 1872. An earlier version of the story had it that his master was Jock Gray, a farmer who regularly dined near Greyfriars'. When Jock died Bobby continued to visit the dining room for his food and spent the rest of his day guarding his master's grave in the kirkyard. This went on for fourteen years and inspired Eleanor Atkinson to write his story in 1912, a book which has been in print ever since.

Turn sharply to the left here , cross George IV Bridge and pass the National Library. Turn right at Deacon Brodie's Tavern into High Street . Deacon Brodie was hung in 1788 for burglary. Although seeming to be an honest and religious man, he was really the leader of a daring gang of housebreakers. Robert Louis Stevenson may have modelled the diverse characters of Dr Jeckyll and Mr Hyde from that of Brodie.

The High Street forms the main part of the Royal Mile which leads from Edinburgh Castle to Holyrood Palace. In rapid succession the walker will pass many of Scotland's most famous sights beginning with St Giles Cathedral, an historic church dating from the 12th century which has suffered many additions and alterations since. Its Thistle Chapel is exceptional being an early 20th century addition in Gothic revival style. Parliament Square lies behind 'the High Kirk'. The Scottish parliament met here until 1707 but after this the buildings were altered in order to accommodate Scotland's judges and advocates.

The classically-styled City Chambers face St Giles from the other

Dean Village

side of the High Street. Look into the various openings off High Street (named Closes, Lands and Wynds) to see reminders of Edinburgh's medieval town plan. Because of lack of space buildings were confined and had to grow upwards rather than outwards. Their height amazed visitors – one building grew to fourteen stories.

Cross North/South Bridge to descend to John Knox House, certainly the most picturesque of the houses in the Old Town. It was built at the beginning of the 16th century and John Knox, the father of the Reformation in Scotland, used to harangue the crowds from its bay window. At the next junction glance down Jeffrey Street for a fine view of Calton Hill.

The other side of this junction marks the start of Canongate which, as its name implies, was connected with the clergy who entered the city this way from their abbey of Holyrood. Before the building of the New Town Canongate was the most fashionable address for the gentry, though it later declined into a slum until its fortunes were revived by 20th-century tourism. The Tolbooth was built at the height of Canongate's prosperity in 1591 when the district was independent of the rest of Edinburgh. This lasted until 1856 when Canongate, with Leith, was incorporated into the city. The Tolbooth we see today was remodelled in 1879 in romantic German gothic idiom. On the other side of the road is the 16th-century Huntly House, once the town house of the first Marquess of Huntly. It now houses the local history museum.

A few steps beyond the Tolbooth is Canongate Kirk, dating from 1691 when James VII forced the congregation of Holyrood Abbey Kirk to find a new place of worship. Adam Smith is amongst many famous people buried in the kirkyard.

Turn back from the Kirk to the Tolbooth and go down Old Tolbooth Wynd ●. Cross the road at the bottom and climb the steps on the other side. Turn left before the top and climb on to reach Regent Road. The imposing façade of the so-called Old Parliament building (formerly a High School) faces you. Turn left to pass the driveway to Calton Hill used by vehicles and walk downhill for 250 yards (228m) to steps on the right ●. Climb a further set of steeper steps which lead off these, also to the right, to reach the top of the hill. There is an excellent view of the city from the base of Nelson's Monument tower but an even better one from the top. The National Monument, Burns' Monument and City Observatory also occupy the summit of the hill. Walk clockwise around the summit to pass the Observatory and take a zigzag path which begins its descent from below the triangulation pillar (the vista northwards is best from here).

Turn sharp right at a broader path to descend to street level by steps opposite John Lewis department store and emerge on Royal Terrace by Greenside church ●. Cross the road and descend through trees to London Road to cross it at traffic lights. Cross Leith Walk and turn left to walk up to York Place passing a church dedicated to Ss Paul and George. There is a fine Georgian vista down Dublin Street which confirms that you are now back in the New Town. The National Portrait Gallery is on the other side of the road as you come to Queen Street, whose southern side has the longest unbroken length of Georgian architecture in the city and which was designed to balance Princes Street on the other side of the New Town. Turn left down Hanover Street ● to return to Princes Street and then left again back to the Scott Monument. ●

Gamelshiel Castle and Whiteadder Water

Start	Western end of Whiteadder Reservoir
Distance	4½ miles (7.2km)
Approximate time	2 hours
Parking	Small car park on left after crossing bridge at western end of Whiteadder Reservoir
Refreshments	None
Ordnance Survey maps	Landranger 67 (Duns, Dunbar & Eyemouth area), Explorer 345 (Lammermuir Hills, Dalkeith, Bonnyrigg & Gifford)

Only two walls remain of Gamelshiel Castle which stands in a remote position below Spartleton Hill in the Lammermuirs. Although little is known of its history its stones speak eloquently of centuries of hardship and suffering. After the castle the route follows a track that strikes northwards across lonely moorland. The return is via the The Herring Road, a footpath close to the delightful Whiteadder Water.

The road between Gifford and Duns (B6355) crosses the northern arm of the Whiteadder Reservoir over a causeway and at the eastern end of the latter there is a small car park and a gate across a track which heads north. Walk up this

The crumbling walls of Gamelshiel Castle

track to a sheepfold (marked as Sheep Wash on the map). Fork right here **Ⓐ** to follow the Hall Burn up to the castle **Ⓑ** whose crumbling walls frame a typical view of the Lammermuirs with Mayshiel the farm in the distance.

The energetic will be tempted to climb to the summit of Spartleton Hill from this point but be warned that it is a stiff climb over rough ground from here and is better approached from Gamelshiel Farm to the east. Our route fords Hall Burn (wearers of shorts should be warned that the castle is surrounded by nettlebeds) and then takes a footpath northwards which gradually climbs the western flank of

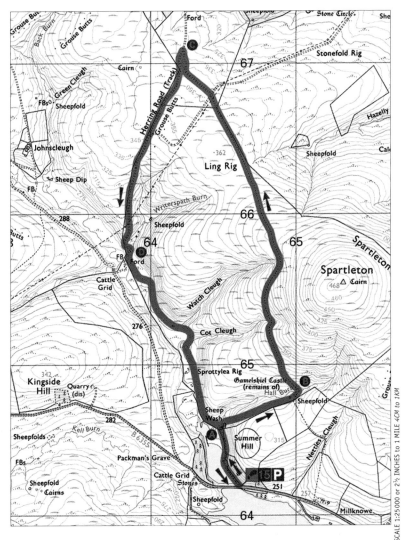

Spartleton Hill. The walking is good on the grassy path which runs just below the line where heather and bracken take over.

Beyond the top of Watch Cleugh the path becomes more faint. Fork right here to pass through a line of butts and continue to head towards electric lines when a fence is joined to the right. Pass beneath the lines and keep walking ahead on a good track to reach a fence and then join The Herring Road (*see* page 84).

Turn left here ● to pass beneath the cables again and descend on the track which goes round a sharp hairpin near the bottom. Before the gate leave the track ● by turning left to cross Writerspath Burn and take a beautiful grassy track on the left bank of Whiteadder Water. There is a wonderful choice of places to picnic or paddle and the marshy ground near the head of the reservoir is the habitat of many unusual plants. All too soon the sheepfold encountered at the start of the walk comes into view ●. Retrace your steps from here on the track which returns to the little car park.

●

Monynut Edge

Start	Upper Monynut Forest, where road descends to Monynut Water
Distance	5½ miles (8.9km)
Approximate time	3 hours
Parking	At start
Refreshments	None
Ordnance Survey maps	Landranger 67 (Duns, Dunbar and Eyemouth area) Explorer 345 (Lammermuir Hills, Dalkeith, Bonnyrigg & Gifford)

Monynut Edge is a lonely corner of the northern Lammermuirs with its western slopes mainly covered by forest. A good track goes through the forest and gives enjoyable walking. After leaving the forest the route climbs rough ground to join a track to reach Packman's Grave and then descends to the road. The varied terrain and the isolation of these beautiful hills makes this a memorable walk but the return leg should only be undertaken in clear conditions.

The walk starts from the point where the road going eastwards through the forest crosses Monynut Water. Take the forest track which climbs the side of the hill on the eastern side of the burn and climbs gently southeastwards. It begins to descend when it reaches a point opposite a white house on the other side of the valley (Upper Monynut). It crosses the burn Ⓐ and climbs again. There are excellent views of Monynut Edge and Heart Law which the walker will climb later.

When the track swings sharply to the right Ⓑ at a hairpin bend leave it by turning left down a heathery firebreak where there is a distinct path. Near the bottom this goes through dense and prickly young pine trees. Persevere to reach the stream and cross it close to the fence Ⓒ – you may have to take boots off after wet weather.

Now head northwards to climb Camy Cleugh Rig, crossing the burn and taking the clearest sheep path. This will be hard work but soon Short Crib Burn, a formidable gully, should come into view on the left. The track going to Packman's Grave runs close to the top of the gully and one of the meandering sheeptracks will take you to it as you keep heading northwards Ⓓ.

The track maintains the northerly direction and there are fine views down

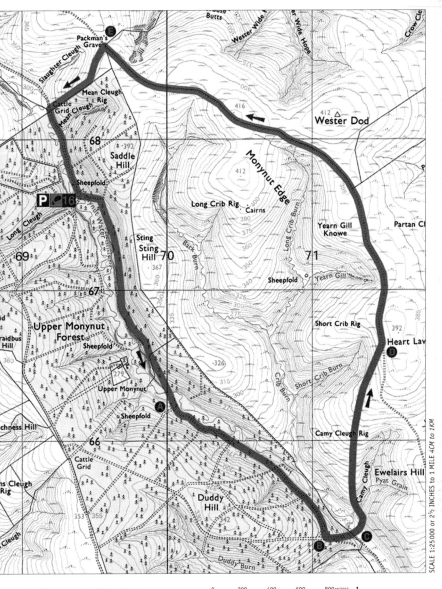

to the forest to the left. This is an exhilarating ridge walk but the track becomes fainter when it meets a fence below Wester Dod. The triangulation pillar on the summit (1352ft/412m) may be clearly seen through a gateway. After the next gate the track more or less disappears. Continue to walk by the fence. There is a radio mast to the right and just to the left of this the cement works on the coast near Dunbar can be clearly seen.

There is no sign of Packman's Grave at the point where the track meets two fences **E**. Although nothing survives to tell us who the peddler was or how he died the map bestows an aura of sadness to the spot.

From the site of the grave descend close to the forest to the road and turn left. A few minutes of pleasant walking brings you back to the road bridge across Monynut Water. ●

River Almond Walk

Start	Mid Calder near Livingston
Distance	6½ miles (10.5km)
Approximate time	3½ hours
Parking	Country Park car park on south side of bridge at Mid Calder
Refreshments	Light refreshments at Almondell Country Park Centre. Pubs in Mid Calder
Ordnance Survey maps	Landranger 65 (Falkirk & Linlithgow, Dunfermline), Explorer 350 (Edinburgh, Musselburgh & Queensferry)

The delightful walk by the River Almond through Almondell Country Park is at the heart of this route which continues on a footpath above the river to Lin's Mill. Here it joins the Union Canal and crosses the Almond on a spectacular aqueduct which may not suit those with a dislike of heights. The way back to Mid Calder is on country lanes and different paths through the Country Park.

Leave the car park at Mid Calder on a footpath and turn right by the Country Park sign to cross a bridge over Murieston Water. A steep climb follows to reach the top of the valley of the River Almond. The unglamorous sewage plant is largely screened by trees and the views towards the river and the weir are a fine distraction. Cross the footbridge and walk close to the canal feeder stream. This accompanies the walker for most of the outward route and was built between 1818 and 1823 to serve the Union Canal between Edinburgh and Falkirk. The infamous body snatchers, Burke and Hare, were employed as navvies on the construction of the canal.

The path passes beneath a fine viaduct which was built in 1885 for a railway to nearby brickworks and limeworks. The line closed in 1956. Keep ahead to pass the footbridge bearing the aqueduct unless you wish to visit the riverside picnic site (the return leg of the walk is on the east bank of the river at this point).

Keep ahead too at lovely Almondell

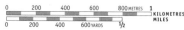

Bridge  to cross the drive on to a lower path close to the river. The bridge was built in 1800 by Alexander Naysmith who was also a talented landscape artist and painted the only authentic portrait of Robert Burns. A small bridge crosses a burn and an old stone records that it was built in 1784 by Margaret, Countess of Buchan. This part of the walk is glorious in autumn.

The path passes the Visitor Centre whose shop provides tea and coffee (but is closed between noon and 1pm). There are picnic tables and barbecue facilities as well as toilets.

Continue on the riverside path to cross the suspension bridge B and climb to turn left on to a path which strikes westwards above the riverbank (do not climb up the steps). Climb a stile

Almondell Bridge, East Calder

and walk with the feeder stream to the right. Cross a lane and follow the sign to Lin's Mill Aqueduct. Many more stiles are crossed but the path is grassy and there are wide views. Eventually the path enters a wood and then divides as it passes beneath electric lines ⓒ. Go left here and cross the canal feeder in a meadow where it emerges through a brick portal and then take the path along its left-hand bank.

The route is now straightforward as it follows the feeder stream which occasionally vanishes underground for short sections. There are glimpses of the river far below – the grand house opposite is Illieston, originally a royal hunting lodge but remodelled as a residence in 1665. After crossing a track and a very high stile the path carries on by the stream until a high viaduct comes into view – this is the aqueduct which takes the Union Canal across the Almond Valley. Soon afterwards you climb steps to a lane. Turn left and keep left when the lane divides to pass beneath the aqueduct ⓓ. There used to be a mill on the river at this point owned by William Lin, who in 1645 was the last man to die of plague in Scotland.

Go up the steps to the right of the green gate to the north towpath and cross the aqueduct. In 1895 an enormous icicle grew from an arch of the viaduct to reach the surface of the river 120ft (36m) below. Certainly the height is spectacular and may not be to everyone's taste. When the towpath reaches the other side there is a section where its original granite setts are still to be seen.

Cross the canal at the first bridge ⓔ and walk down a track to join a road at Muirend. Pass a property named Lookaboutye and, on the left, a drive to Drumshoreland House and turn left at crossroads on to the driveway into the Country Park. This takes you directly to the Visitor Centre which stands on the site of Almondell House, built c.1790 by Henry Erskine, brother of the 11th earl of Buchan. He designed it himself but proved to be a poor architect – the roof leaked, foundations became waterlogged, and timber shrank because it was not properly seasoned. He even built the icehouse facing south! Consequently the mansion became dangerously dilapidated, finally being pulled down in 1969.

Follow the drive past the Visitor Centre (the astronomical pillar in front is from another Erskine home nearby, Kirkhill House at Broxburn) and cross Almondell Bridge ⓐ. Take the path on the right after the bridge which skirts a grassy picnic area by the river. Do not cross the suspension bridge but climb steps to walk high above the river. Unfortunately you have to lose height to cross a mini-ravine and then regain it by climbing steps to the railway viaduct. Crossing this gives a spectacular view of the valley. Descend steps to the left on the far side of the viaduct and turn right on to the path at the bottom. You are now on the path next to the canal stream used earlier and it is easy to retrace your steps back to the starting point. ⬤

Pencaitland and Ormiston

Start	West Saltoun, 6½ miles south of Haddington
Distance	6½ miles (10.5km)
Approximate time	3 hours
Parking	At start
Refreshments	Pubs at Easter Pencaitland and Ormiston
Ordnance Survey maps	Landranger 66 (Edinburgh, Penicuik & North Berwick), Explorer 345 (Lammermuir Hills, Dalkeith, Bonnyrigg & Gifford)

The walk starts within a mile of the Glenkinichie distillery which must be a point in its favour. For much of the way it follows the trackbed of an abandoned railway but on the outward section it diverts at Pencaitland on to a pastoral right of way which gives a view of Winton House, built c.1620 and an outstanding example of Renaissance architecture.

An old signal (its arm missing) marks the start of the walk opposite the small parking area ½ mile (800m) to the south-west of West Saltoun. An information board offers an account of the short life of the line. It was opened in 1901 primarily to serve the East Lothian coal field. In 1927 there were three passenger trains on weekdays in

each direction but the line closed to passengers in 1933. Freight traffic ceased in 1964 and the track pulled up soon afterwards. However, the observant walker will be able to spot a few sleepers with rail-chairs still attached, especially at the northern end of the route.

The walk begins with a shady stretch through a cutting but after this the line begins to climb steadily and there are

Winton House

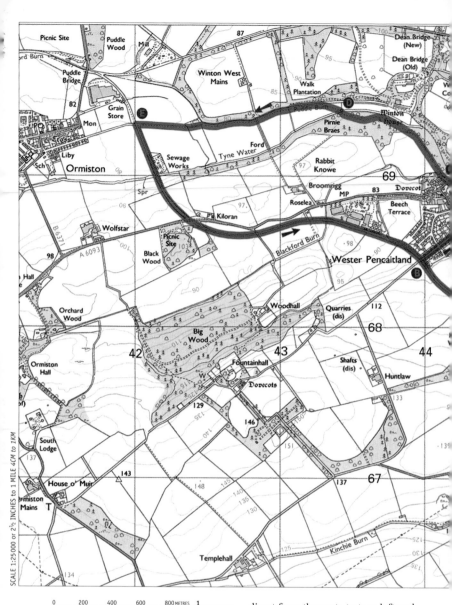

SCALE 1:25000 or 2½ INCHES to 1 MILE 4CM to 1KM

fine views over the countryside from an embankment with the Lammermuir hills off in the distance. A remarkable feature of this walk is the number of cherry trees by the side of the line. In spring the blossom is a feast for the eyes, later you may feast of the fruit left by the birds.

The line goes under two bridges early in the walk. At the second Ⓐ you may divert from the route to turn left and left again to visit Glenkinichie Distillery which has a Visitor Centre etc. On the main route the walking surface is generally excellent but it is as well to be aware that cyclists also use the track and can approach at speed giving little warning. As you come to the first houses in Pencaitland there is a stone on the left with virtually indecipherable lettering, only the words 'South Easter Mine, Haddington' being clear. The shaft of this mine, on the edge of the

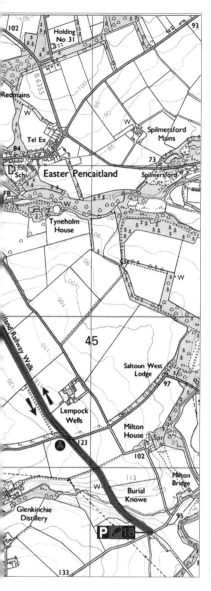

at crossways to walk down a drive to the main road connecting the two parts of the village. Cross this road at the traffic lights to a path on the right bearing a signpost put up by the Scottish Rights of Way Society pointing to Ormiston .

This proves to be a pleasant field path with woodland to the right. Winton House can soon be seen to the right. This was built *c.*1620 by William Wallace, the royal master mason, for George, 8th Lord Seton and 3rd Earl of Winton. It is amongst the finest Renaissance-style houses in Britain, its most remarkable external feature being the tall chimneys with their spiral carving which are as elaborate as those of the finest Jacobean houses in England.

The path threads through the trees, and may be difficult to follow in places. When it divides branch right to descend to the Tyne Water where there is a footbridge over the burn. Turn left to cross the field diagonally to the stream on the far side (Puddle Burn). The footpath runs along the south bank of the burn and, though the path is fenced off, going may be difficult due to long grass and thistles. The right of way leaves the Puddle Burn at a plantation (not marked on the map) and becomes a field path before reaching the old railway line again just outside Ormiston . Turn left on to it to continue the walk or turn right to see the village.

The way back to West Saltoun is straightforward and makes enjoyable walking. A large grainstore occupies the site of Pencaitland station and there is a 1 in 50 climb up from this point which the firemen on the locomotives must have dreaded. There are opportunities of refreshment from trackside cherries and blackberries, or the walker may choose to divert to the distillery for refreshment and a guided tour. ●

East Lothian coal field, was situated close by. Today it seems incredible that at the beginning of the 20th century Pencaitland and Ormiston were busy mining villages comparable to those of South Wales or Yorkshire.

Leave the track to the right at the next bridge and walk down to the end of Huntlaw Road. Cross the road at this T-junction to an enclosed footpath on the other side which joins a driveway to a nursing home. Turn left and immediately right, and then left again

Caerketton and Allermuir Hills

Start	Hillend Ski Centre Country Park
Distance	4½ miles (7.25km)
Approximate time	2½ hours
Parking	Hillend Ski Centre
Refreshments	Café at Ski Centre, pub at Hillend
Ordnance Survey maps	Landranger 66 (Edinburgh & Midlothian), Explorer 350 (Edinburgh, Musselburgh & Queensferry)

The smooth, grassy slopes of the Pentland Hills to the south-west of Edinburgh provide excellent and quite demanding walking right on the edge of the city. This walk starts with a steep climb beside the Hillend artificial ski-slope to the summit of Caerketton Hill (1,502ft/458m) and then continues along a switchback ridge to the higher Allermuir Hill (1,618ft/493m). All the way there are magnificent and extensive views. After an easy descent, the return to Hillend takes you through the picturesque hamlet of Swanston.

From the car park take the steep uphill path, lined by wire fences to the right of the ski-slope and alongside a golf-course on the right. Climb a stile in the top corner of the golf-course, continue uphill across grass in the same direction as before – do not turn right alongside the golf-course fence or bear left to continue by a wire fence on the left – and, on meeting an obvious path, turn sharp left Ⓐ and continue uphill, re-joining the wire fence bordering the ski-slope.

Follow the path up to the top of the ski-slope. Shortly afterwards it curves to the right away from the fence, heading more steeply uphill to meet a wire fence. Turn right alongside it up to a small cairn, descend and then climb again to reach the cairn on the summit of Caerketton Hill. The extensive views

include Edinburgh, Arthur's Seat, Lothian coast, Bass Rock, the Lammermuir Hills, the rest of the Pentlands and across the Firth of Forth to the hills of Fife.

Continue, alongside a wire fence on the left, along a winding and roller-coaster path across the smooth, grassy, heathery slopes, finally ascending steeply to the triangulation pillar and the National Trust for Scotland's view indicator on Allermuir Hill Ⓑ. This is another magnificent viewpoint.

Retrace your steps down into the first dip, where the path forks, and here leave the outward route to continue along the left-hand path that winds downhill between rough grass and heather, keeping below the sheer face of Caerketton Craigs on the right. At a junction of paths, just before reaching

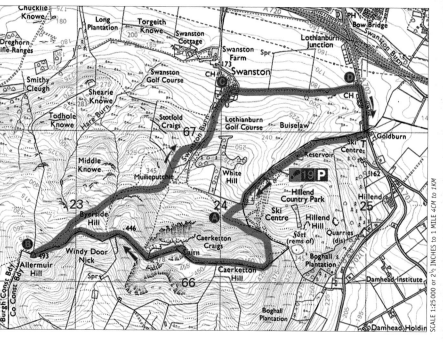

the corner of the golf-course, turn left at a waymarked post along a grassy path between gorse bushes. Arthur's Seat can be seen ahead in the distance. Take the right-hand, lower path at the next fork, continuing downhill between gorse and trees, and to the right is the aptly named T Wood, planted in the shape of a Greek cross in 1766 as a memorial to a member of the Trotter family who died in battle.

Swanston village

The path bends right and heads down to a kissing-gate. Go through and follow it as it first bends to the right, then curves to the left to cross a footbridge over the tiny Swanston Burn, and curves left again, by a waymarked post, to continue down into Swanston village. As a boy, the writer Robert Louis Stevenson used to stay in this delightful hamlet of thatched and whitewashed cottages, which is situated on the lower slopes of the Pentlands.

Go through a kissing-gate, keep ahead between cottages and then turn right **C** along a tarmac drive. Go through another kissing-gate, continue along a track beside the left-hand edge of the golf-course, by a wire fence on the left, and go through a kissing-gate onto the main road **D**. Turn right and, at the entrance to Hillend Ski Centre Country Park, turn right again to return to the starting point of the walk. ●

Priestlaw Hill from Whiteadder Reservoir

Start	West end of Whiteadder Reservoir on B6355 about 7 miles east of Gifford
Distance	6 miles (9.7km)
Approximate time	3½ hours
Parking	Roadside parking before cattle-grid
Refreshments	None
Ordnance Survey maps	Pathfinder 422, NT 66/76 (Abbey St Bathans), Explorer 345 (Lammermuir Hills, Dalkieth, Bonnyriff & Gifford)

The outward part of the route is easy walking on a track, grassy at times, following Faseny Water. This burn is one of the scenic delights of a walk into lonely countryside where it will be a surprise to meet other walkers. The return begins on a clearly marked path but the descent from the summit of Priestlaw Hill is over rough heather and care is needed for ankles as well as navigation.

Take the lane which heads south past the top of the reservoir signposted to Priestlaw Farm. Turn right Ⓐ before the bridge towards Penshiel. Just before the white bungalow turn right through a gate on to a hill track which climbs steadily away from the reservoir. In a field to the left of the track are the scant remains of a monks' grange (probably belonging to Abbey St Bathans, less than ten miles to the east) while to the right is a chapel stone, a reminder of religious persecution in former times when catholics were forced to worship in remote locations. The track is level and grassy for a while and the walker will encounter curlews, skylarks and grouse as well as innumerable rabbits.

The track soon becomes stony again though the walking is most enjoyable with Faseny Water below to the left. There are some delightful picnic sites on its banks. Continue walking southwards and turn left when you reach the road Ⓑ.

The road climbs steeply and serves as the county boundary for part of this stretch. After

Whiteadder Reservoir

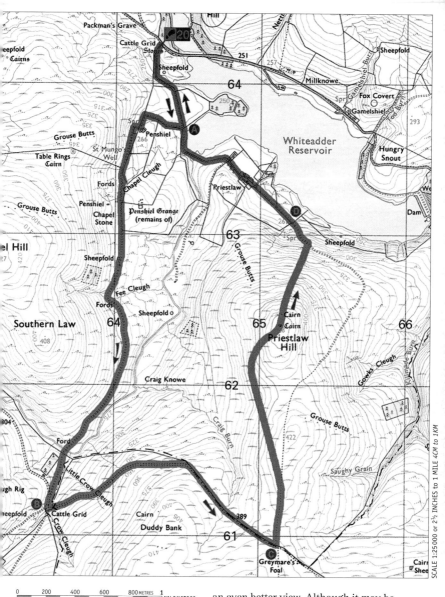

about 1 mile (1.6km), and just after the summit of the climb, there is a gate on the left **C**. Go through this and bear left when the track divides to follow a rough track marked with wooden posts which climbs the western flank of Priestlaw Hill. The track leads to a point below the extensive summit cairn. Climb up to this and then continue north to a smaller cairn which provides an even better view. Although it may be thought easiest to descend from the hill via the continuation of the track that has brought you there, the landowner prefers walkers to descend from the hill down its heather-covered northern slopes. Head to the right of the farm where a gate **D** leads into the pastures – take care over the rough ground.

Having passed through the gate walk down the track and go through the farmyard. Cross the bridge and then climb back to the starting point. ●

Hailes Castle and Traprain Law

Start	East Linton
Distance	6½ miles (10.5km). Shorter version 3½ miles (5.5km)
Approximate time	3½ hours (2 hours for shorter version)
Parking	Around The Square at East Linton
Refreshments	Pubs and cafés at East Linton
Ordnance Survey maps	Landranger 67 (Duns, Dunbar & Eyemouth), Explorer 346 (Berwick-upon-Tweed, Eyemouth & Duns)

A pleasant footpath along the banks of the River Tyne leads from East Linton to the attractively sited ruins of Hailes Castle. From here the shorter version returns directly to East Linton along a quiet lane, but the full walk takes in Traprain Law (725ft/221m), the distinctive, conical-shaped hill that rises abruptly above the lowlands of East Lothian and which can be seen for miles around. Apart from the short but steep climb to the summit of Traprain Law, this is an easy and fairly flat walk.

The walk starts in the Square by the church. Walk down Bridge Street to a T-junction, turn right under a railway bridge and a few yards ahead turn sharp left at a notice 'Private Road, Pedestrian Right of Way only', along a tarmac track that heads down to the river. Turn right at the bottom onto the riverside path.

Pass under the A1 to continue along this most attractive, narrow path beside the River Tyne. Part of the route is through woodland. At one stage you climb steps above the river – from where there is a lovely view of the Tyne below and Traprain Law in the background – later descending steps to rejoin the riverbank, to continue along the edge of sloping meadows. Climb a stile to walk through some more trees, passing below a sheer cliff-face to reach a footbridge by Hailes Mill Ⓐ. Turn left over it and follow the uphill path ahead to a lane. Keep ahead along the lane to the mainly 13th-century remains of Hailes Castle, formerly the seat of the earls of Bothwell, which occupy a fine position above the river. Mary Queen of Scots stayed here in 1567 as the new wife of James Hepburn, Earl of Bothwell; he was her third husband and one of the conspirators involved in the murder of her second husband, Darnley.

The shorter walk returns along this quiet, narrow lane to East Linton, rejoining the full walk at Ⓖ.

Just before reaching the castle, turn left Ⓑ along a track in front of a house, pass beside a metal gate and continue between trees. After emerging from the woodland, the track ascends and bends to the right to continue between a wall

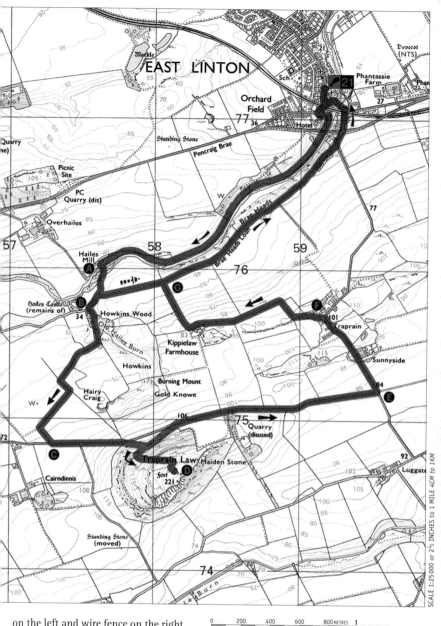

on the left and wire fence on the right. follow it around several bends, at a fork turn left along a hedge-lined track and pass beside a metal gate onto a road **C**. Turn left towards Traprain Law, heading gently uphill.

Climb a stile on the right, bear left and follow the fairly clear path that zigzags steeply uphill – there are several footpath markers – to the summit of Traprain Law **D**. The steep climb is well

worth the effort because the magnificent view from the triangulation pillar and summit cairn encompasses a long stretch of the Lothian coast from Dunbar to the Firth of Forth, the fertile Lothian lowlands and the line of the Lammermuir and Pentland hills. The summit is crowned by an Iron Age hill-fort, the headquarters of the Votadini tribe who inhabited most of south-eastern Scotland. The Votadini apparently collaborated with the Roman conquerors, and the fort seems to have been used continuously up to the fifth century AD, when it was abandoned around the time that the Angles moved into the area. In 1919 a remarkable hoard of Roman silver was found here.

Descend from the summit but at the bottom – before reaching the stile used earlier – turn right along a path that keeps parallel to the wall and road on the left. Climb a stile in the wall corner and descend steps onto the road by a parking-area. Turn right along the road for nearly 1 mile (1.5km), at a T-junction **E** turn left gently uphill and at a right-hand bend turn left **F** along a narrow lane, signposted Kippielaw. Follow it around several sharp bends as it descends to a T-junction **G** and turn right along a narrow lane above the winding River Tyne as far as another T-junction.

Turn left, cross the A1, continue along the road opposite down into East Linton, passing under a railway bridge to a T-junction.

Turn left to cross a bridge over the river, follow the road to the left and, before reaching a railway bridge, turn right up Bridge Street to return to the Square. ●

The remains of Hailes Castle

Huntly Cot Hills and Hirendean Castle

Start	From eastern side of Gladhouse Reservoir
Distance	7½ miles (12km)
Approximate time	4½ hours
Parking	Layby on eastern side of road about ½ mile from Gladhouse (just after junction)
Refreshments	None
Ordnance Survey maps	Landranger 66 (Edinburgh, Penicuik & North Berwick), Explorer 344 (Pentland Hills, Penicuik & West Linton)

The drive around the reservoir to the starting point is not the least of the scenic delights of this route in the Moorfoot Hills, particularly if you are there early in the morning and the sun is shining. The going is over rough ground at times but once on the hills you are unlikely to meet other walkers and the silence is only disturbed by aircraft, birdsong, and the wind in the heather. Ask locally if you intend to walk the route during the grouse shooting season (12 August–10 December).

Continue southwards along the road to pass an Arniston Estates signboard which warns that dogs are not welcome on the land. Before Mauldslie go through the gate ahead when faced with a T-junction Ⓐ. Climb up the grassy track with the burn to the right to reach a small clump of trees. It is worth pausing here to take in the view back.

Go through the gate at the top and bear slightly left on a faint path heading towards a plantation. The ford shown on the map ● is midway between the plantation on the left and a small hillock to the right. After the ford the path leads to the top corner of the plantation. From here a clear path climbs gradually up the flank of the hill in an easterly direction heading for a point above another small plantation.

Huntly Cot

Cross another burn and walk along the edge of bracken, climbing steadily. Having left the plantation behind, a fence comes into view ahead. Climb with this to the left to reach a gate where two fences meet ●.

Having gone through the gate turn right to follow the fence south-westwards. You are walking on the boundary between the Lothians and the Borders. A track runs by the fence for most of the way on Mauldslie Hill and there are magnificent views westwards over the reservoir. The view to the left is

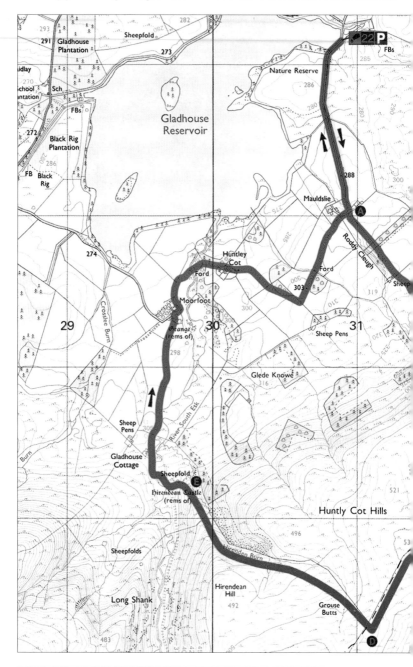

of lonely, softly moulded hills with no paths or tracks obvious. A fence comes up from the right. Continue on the path which grows ever fainter to cross the Huntly Cot Hills where the imperceptible summit is at 1742ft (531m).

When a second fence joins on the right, pass through (or over) the gate 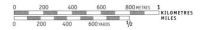 and walk down over rough heather with the fence to the right. Pass to the right of butts taking care over moist, tussocky ground. A burn steadily grows in strength to the right and provides pools whose cool waters will soothe aching feet. A path becomes discernible by the burn though this probably owes more to sheep than to man.

Take care when the descent becomes steep and rocky with the stream passing to the other side of the fence and dropping down cascades. The path is now clear and the ruins of Hirendean Castle now come into view. Pass both the castle ● and the circular brick-built sheep fold and then descend to the track. Turn right on to this track and cross the burn.

The track leads to Moorfoot farmyard. Bear right here to follow the signpost to Huntly Cottage. The remainder of the route is on well-signed farm tracks leading back to Mauldslie and the road which takes you back to the start.   ●

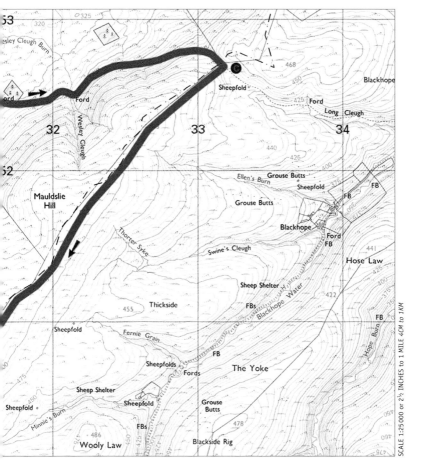

Loganlea and Glencorse Reservoirs with Scald Law

Loganlea and Glencorse Reservoirs with Scald Law

Start	Flotterstone Glen Countryside Information Centre, off A702 2 miles north east of Penicuik
Distance	7½ miles (12km) 6½ miles (10.5km) alternative route
Approximate time	5 hours (4 hours alternative route)
Parking	At start
Refreshments	Pub at start
Ordnance Survey maps	Landranger 66 (Edinburgh, Penicuik & North Berwick) Explorer 344 (Pentland Hills, Penicuik & West Linton)

The outward section of this Pentland walk is demanding, entailing a steep ascent and then a switchback ridge walk. The the finale of the longer route is the ascent of Scald Law (1898ft/579m). The way back is a level walk by the shores of the two reservoirs with fine views of the hills traversed earlier. Note: The route should not be attempted if visibility is poor.

Turn right from the car park to head towards Glencorse Reservoir and join a footpath on the right that winds through trees by the side of the road. The path passes a plaque dedicated to C.T.R. Wilson who was born nearby at Crosshouse Farm in 1869. Wilson was a pioneer of atomic and nuclear physics who was a Nobel Prize winner and inventor of the cloud chamber which assisted the study of atoms and electrons. Soon the path merges with the road and 50 yards (46m) further on a path leaves on the left waymarked to Scald Law Ⓐ. Take this, cross the bridge and bear right following a purple Pentland Way waymark. The broad grassy track is the start of a lengthy climb of about 1300ft (396m), though due to the switchback nature of the ridge the overall height to be climbed is considerably greater than this. Unnecessary effort is saved early on by

keeping left on lower paths.

Most people will take a breather by the topmost trees from where there is a fine view back. Within 30 minutes from the start of the walk the first summit may be reached (though don't worry if you fail this arbitrary target). This is Turnhouse Hill with its cairn at 1660ft (506m). It provides a spectacular view through 360°, though Glencorse Reservoir is completely hidden.

Descend White Craig Heads to the wall Ⓑ before beginning another stiff ascent to the top of Carnethy Hill at 1879ft (573m). The stone-strewn summit gives a good view of Glencorse Reservoir but now Loganlea is hidden.

Continue on the ridge path by dropping down to the col Ⓒ where a path from Penicuik joins from the south east. Edinburgh and the Forth can be seen to the north through a gap in the hills. If you have had enough climbing

Glencorse

by now turn right off the ridge path on to the Kirk Road, descend directly to the head of Loganlea Reservoir ⑥, and then turn right along the road to complete the shorter route and return to Flotterstone.

The complete route entails a brisk

climb to the top of Scald Law, at 1898ft (579m) the highest of the Pentland summits covered on this walk. On reaching the top, pause to study the terrain from here and note particularly the plantation to the west and the gully lower down (Lover's Loup). The descending route is on the west side of the gully and a path can be clearly seen leaving the ridge northwards towards the wood.

When the ridge path divides fork right and descend to the col  and there turn right again on a clear path heading north. Go through a gate and continue to descend with a fence to the right. A perfect view of both Glencorse and Loganlea reservoirs now comes into view as height is lost with a farmhouse in the foreground to give scale to the

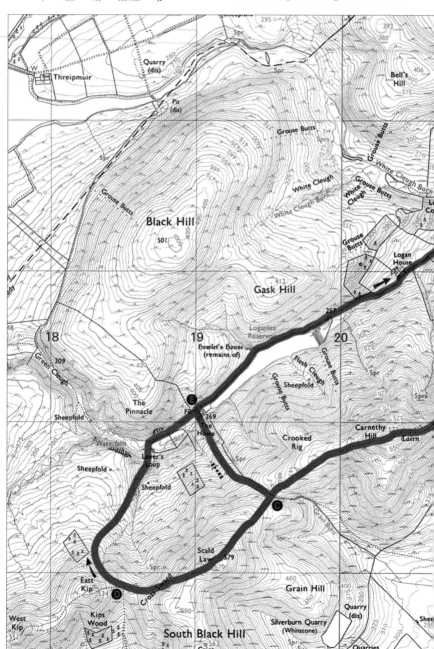

vista. Turn right at the bottom to join the right of way and follow this to the road serving the reservoirs where the shorter route joins **E**.

At weekends the road may be busy with cyclists and anglers' cars. The walk back to the car park will take nearly 90 minutes but is enjoyable for its views of the hills you have walked earlier in the day. For much of the way there are wide grassy verges which are soothing to the feet. One of the great advantages of this walk is that there is a pub at the end of it.

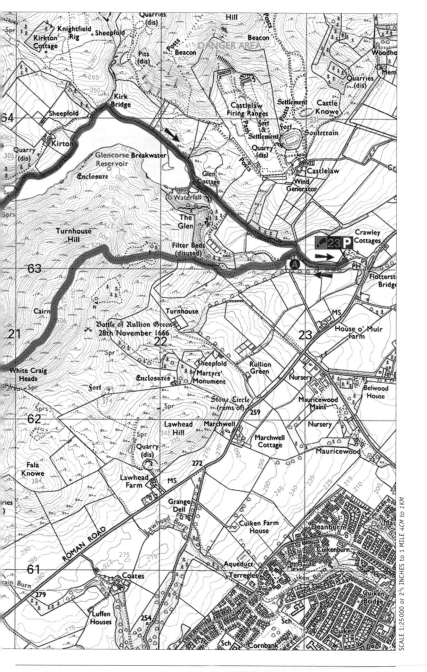

SCALE 1:25000 or 2½ INCHES to 1 MILE 4CM to 1KM

Haddington and the River Tyne

Start	Haddington
Distance	8½ miles (13.5km)
Approximate time	4 hours
Parking	Haddington
Refreshments	Pubs and cafés at Haddington
Ordnance Survey maps	Landranger 66 maps (Edinburgh & Midlothian), Explorer 351 (Dunbar & North Berwick, Musselburgh)

After a steady climb along a road onto the lower slopes of the Garleton Hills, the route continues along a track and lane, with fine views across the Tyne valley to the Lammermuirs, later descending to join a disused railway track. The next stage of the walk follows the track for just over 2½ miles (4km) to the edge of Haddington and, after a short section through a modern housing area, the final stretch is a delightful walk beside the placid, tree-lined River Tyne.

Haddington Church

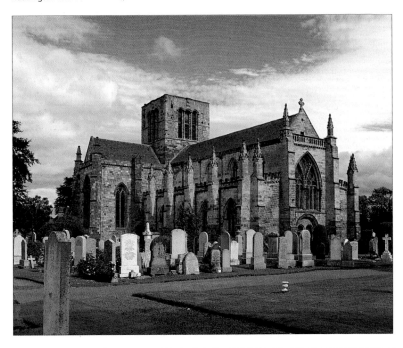

The River Tyne at Haddington

Many handsome and dignified 18th- and early 19th-century houses reflect the former prosperity of Haddington, which lies in the centre of some of the most fertile agricultural land in Scotland. The most impressive building is the 14th- and 15th-century collegiate church of St Mary, cathedral-like both in its design and proportions, with a fine west front and spacious interior. It has a most attractive setting, overlooking a bend in the River Tyne and the picturesque 16th-century Nungate Bridge.

Start at the 18th-century town house and walk along Market Street to a crossroads and traffic lights. Turn left and walk up Hardgate to Dunbar Road and follow the main road right to a roundabout. Keep ahead here to reach another roundabout after passing beneath a bridge. Take the exit, the road to Dream and Camptoun, climbing steadily.

Just before reaching the top of this road, turn left Ⓐ along a path that soon becomes attractively hedge- and tree-lined, with fine views to the left over the Tyne valley to the Lammermuir Hills. On the hill to the right is the Hopetoun Monument. The path later broadens out into a track to reach a road. Cross over, continue along the lane ahead and, where it bears left downhill, take the narrow lane to the right Ⓑ and follow that downhill. Turn right at a T-junction, continue around several sharp bends, turn left Ⓒ at a 'Railway Walk' sign and turn left again into Cottyburn car park.

Turn left Ⓓ onto the track of the disused Long Niddry to Haddington branch of the North British Railway Company, opened in 1846, closed in 1968 and later converted into a cycle and walking track. Follow this pleasant, peaceful, tree-lined track for just over 2¹⁄₂ miles (4km) to the reach the edge of picturesque Haddington, passing under five bridges – including the A1 – and eventually reaching a road by a new housing estate. Cross the road, keep

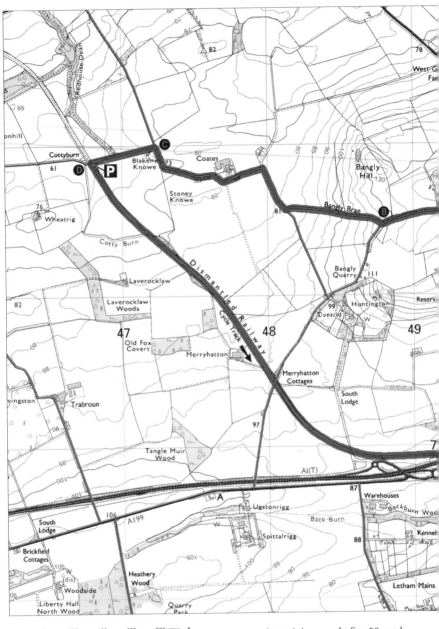

ahead along the track and just before the next bridge, bear left off it and head up to a road **E**. Turn right, cross the bridge and continue down to the main road.

Cross over and take the tarmac track opposite to join a road after 50 yards (46m). Continue along it through a new housing area down to a T-junction, turn left and almost immediately turn right along Long Cram. Follow the road as it curves left and, just after passing a road to the right, look out for a path between garden fences and turn right onto it. The path turns left and continues along

the right-hand edge of an open grassy area, by a wire fence on the right, to reach the River Tyne

Bear left to walk beside a tranquil, mostly tree-lined stretch of the river. After turning right to cross a footbridge by a weir, continue along a tarmac path and cross a road to the left of Waterloo Bridge. Now comes a particularly memorable final section as the river curves to the left around a wide meadow, passing St Mary's Church, to reach Nungate Bridge.

Continue along the road past the bridge, bearing left to a crossroads, keep ahead, passing to the left of the George Hotel, and walk along High Street to the start.

The Shore Walk to Cramond

Start	The Hawes Inn at South Queensferry
Distance	8½ miles (13.5km)
Approximate time	4 hours
Parking	Public car park by Hawes Quay
Refreshments	Pubs at South Queensferry and Cramond
Ordnance Survey maps	Landranger 65 (Falkirk & Linlithgow, Dunfermline), Explorer 350 (Edinburgh, Musselburgh & Queensferry)

The route described here is from South Queensferry; it can equally well be walked from Cramond as long as the ferry is operating. The ferryman has his day off on Friday and may also take a summer holiday, but otherwise the ferry operates throughout the year except at Christmas and Hogmanay. The Shore Path is a concessionary footpath which runs through the Dalmeny Estate.
Please note that dogs are not allowed.

The Hawes Inn is possibly the most famous pub in Scotland, Robert Louis Stevenson having used it as a setting in *Kidnapped*. Walk past the pub and fork left from the main road to pass beneath the piers of the railway bridge. The shoreline track gives wonderful views of the road and railway bridges though mature trees screen the view at times. Go through the white kissing- gate Ⓐ at Long Craig Pier and continue along the shady drive which was obviously made for carriages. The tanker berth just offshore illustrates the enormous length of these vessels. A cleared area shows where the oil or gas pipeline comes ashore and the metalled track ends at this point.

The track climbs to overlook beautiful Peatdraught Bay Ⓑ with its sandy beach. A little further on there are seats on Hound Point which give a fine view of the mouth of the Firth and along the shore to Cramond Island. The bulk of Arthur's Seat to the south-east is another obvious landmark. The track passes the picturesque Fishery Cottage and comes to a second white gate just before Barnbougle Castle. It joins a surfaced drive and there is a glimpse of the renovated castle through a gateway on the left Ⓒ.

The drive leads into Dalmeny Park and there is a very fine view of Dalmeny House. The path leaves the drive to the left Ⓓ and follows the shoreside edge of the golf course. At low tide, miles of mud flats are revealed which are a habitat to flocks of oyster catchers and other waders. From here Cramond Island has the outline of a battleship.

Beyond the golf course the path enters woodland again – the tall pines

Cramond

resemble palms with their tiny umbrellas of foliage at their tops. The track crosses another drive by the cottages at Long Green and then resumes its course through the wood. It climbs to swing round Snab Point and at Hunter's Crag ⬤ the beautiful houses of Cramond are revealed, with their white walls and red roofs. The final stretch of the walk is a delight in high summer with loosestrife and willowherb by the path. Enormous daisies are grown in front of the ferryman's cottage.

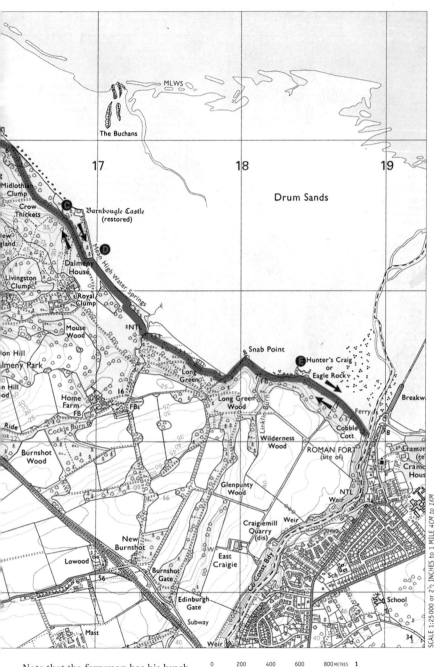

Drum Sands

The Buchans

MLWS

17 18 19

Midlothian Clump

Crow Thickets

Barnbougle Castle (restored)

Dalmeny House

Livingston Clump

Royal Clump

Mouse Wood

NTL

Snab Point

Hunter's Craig or Eagle Rock

Long Green

Long Green Wood

Home Farm

FB

FBs

Cockle Burn

Ride

Burnshot Wood

Wilderness Wood

Cobble Cott

Ferry

Breakw

ROMAN FORT (site of)

Cramo

Cramo Hous

NTL Weir

Glenpunty Wood

Weir

Craigiemill Quarry (dis)

Weir

New Burnshot

East Craigie

Lowood

Burnshot Gate

Sch

School

Edinburgh Gate

Subway

Mast

Weir

34

SCALE 1:25000 or 2½ INCHES to 1 MILE 4CM to 1KM

0   200   400   600   800 METRES   1
                              KILOMETRES
                              MILES
0   200   400   600 YARDS   ½

Note that the ferryman has his lunch between 1pm and 2pm. Timing is vital if you intend to take lunch yourself at Cramond. The walk can be extended for several more miles along the shore from Cramond, or you can take a bus back to Queensferry (check). If you do the walk in the opposite direction Dalmeny Station is close to the Hawes Inn and there are frequent services to Edinburgh.

THE SHORE WALK TO CRAMOND ● 79

Pentland Ridge

Start	Threipmuir Reservoir. From Balerno follow signs to Marchbank, and car park is on the left, near where the road ends
Distance	7½ miles (12km)
Approximate time	4½ hours
Parking	Threipmuir
Refreshments	None
Ordnance Survey maps	Landranger 66 (Edinburgh & Midlothian), Explorer 344 (Pentland Hills, Penicuik & West Linton)

A long, gradual climb from Threipmuir Reservoir across open grassland leads to the main, central ridge of the Pentlands and then follows a splendid but quite strenuous switchback walk over three peaks: West Kip, East Kip and Scald Law (1,898ft/579m), the highest point in the Pentland range. As might be expected, the views from the ridge path – to the left across the Pentlands to the Firth of Forth and to the right across the lowlands to the Lammermuir Hills – are magnificent. The descent from Scald Law is followed by an attractive walk through the narrow and steep-sided valley of Green Cleugh to return to the start. This is a most enjoyable and exhilarating walk with plenty of steep climbing and superb views but definitely one to be avoided in bad weather, especially mist, unless you are experienced in such conditions and able to navigate by using a compass.

Turn left out of the car park along a track and, after a few yards where the track bears left, turn sharp right along a path through trees. On reaching a tarmac drive opposite a notice for Red Moss Nature Reserve, turn left along it to cross Redford Bridge over Threipmuir Reservoir.

Continue along the lovely, uphill beech drive ahead and at a T-junction of tracks Ⓐ turn right, at a public footpath sign Nine Mile Burn and Carlops. After going through a gate, turn left along a drive to a stile, climb it and continue along a track, by a wall

and wire fence bordering woodland on the left, to climb another one. Now follow a track gently uphill, keeping parallel to a wall on the left, onto the open, rolling, heathery expanses of the Pentlands, with grand views of the main Pentland ridge. The track leads up to a gate and footpath sign. Go through, continue to cross a burn and shortly head up more steeply, bending left towards the first of the three summits, West Kip.

On reaching a stile in a wire fence on

The Pentland ridge

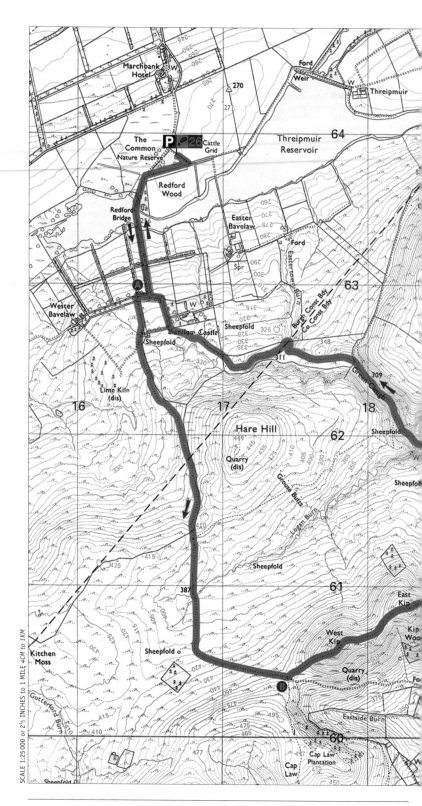

the right, bear left onto a path **B** that heads steeply and dauntingly up the smooth, grassy slopes of West Kip. At the top is the reward of a magnificent view that takes in the Pentland ridge, Firth of Forth, Lothian lowlands and Lammermuir and Moorfoot hills. From here the path descends and then ascends – rather less steeply – to the summit of East Kip. Then follows a steep descent to a fork. Here take the left-hand path to climb steeply again to the triangulation pillar on the summit of Scald Law **C**, the highest point in the Pentlands and an even more magnificent viewpoint.

Continue past the triangulation pillar and head steeply down into the next dip below the slopes of Carnethy Hill. Where paths cross **D**, climb a stile and turn left to head steeply downhill, by a wire fence on the left, to a ladder-stile. Climb it, continue along the path that curves right to another stile, climb that and keep ahead steeply downhill. Nearing the bottom, the path swings left down to a stile. Climb it, by a public footpath sign Old Kirk Road to Penicuik, keep ahead and turn left at a fence corner **E** along a path by a burn on the right. There is a path on each side of the burn – take your pick as either will involve at least one fording.

Continue through the narrow, peaceful, steep-sided valley of Green Cleugh, climbing gently to reach a ladder-stile. Turn left over it to continue along the right-hand side of the valley – the sides are less steep now – climb another ladder-stile and continue towards the trees ahead. The path then turns left to cross two planks over marshy ground and winds past two waymarked posts to a ladder-stile on the edge of the trees, by a public footpath sign Penicuik, Colinton and Flotterstone.

Climb the stile and continue along a beech drive, following it first to the left and shortly around to the right. Here you rejoin the outward route to retrace your steps to the start.　●

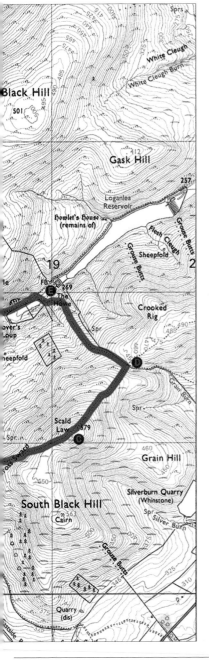

Clints Dod, Herring Road and Dunbar Common

Start	Woodland Trust's Pressmennan Wood car park. From Stenton, take the lane signposted to Deuchrie and, just after Rucklaw West Mains Farm, turn left onto a track at a 'Forest Trail Car Park' sign
Distance	11 miles (17.7km)
Approximate time	5½ hours
Parking	Pressmennan Wood
Refreshments	None
Ordnance Survey maps	Landranger 67 (Duns, Dunbar & Eyemouth) Explorer 346 (Berwick-upon-Tweed, Eyemouth & Duns)

The Lammermuir Hills are a range of rolling, open, heathery moorlands, rising to over 1,700ft (518m) and from their northern slopes there are superb and extensive views over the fertile lowlands of Lothian and along the North Sea coast. This walk over the Lammermuirs is a lengthy but not strenuous walk as all the ascents and descents are long and gradual, and most of the route is along clear and well-surfaced tracks, with just two difficult sections where the track degenerates into a rough, faint and uneven path. It is exhilarating to walk across these wide and empty expanses, and the views are magnificent, but this is a walk best reserved for a fine and clear day; in bad weather and misty conditions route-finding could be difficult in places.

Start by walking back along the track to the lane, turn left and follow it for 1 mile (1.6km) around several sharp bends and over a ford. At a row of cottages on the left, turn left Ⓐ along an uphill tarmac drive to Stoneypath Farm and by the farm turn right through a metal gate, at a public footpath sign to Johnscleugh, to continue along a steadily ascending track. Ahead are grand views over the smooth, heathery slopes of the Lammermuirs, a foretaste of pleasures to come.

Follow the track steadily uphill over Clints Dod. Cross a track just to the right of a house, continue by a wire fence on the left, go through a gate and proceed over the open moorland. After reaching the summit – virtually imperceptible – the track descends gently to a gate. Go through and continue steadily downhill into the Whiteadder valley. Go through a gate, keep ahead to pass between the

0	200	400	600	800 METRES	**1**	
						KILOMETRES
						MILES
0	200	400	600 YARDS	**½**		

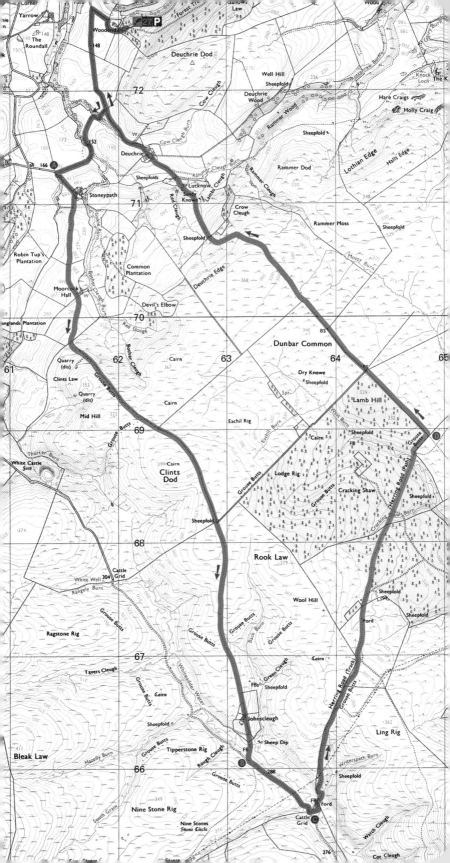

A view of the Lammermuir Hills

buildings of Johnscleugh Farm and continue along a downhill track. Where the track bends sharply to the right, keep ahead steeply downhill, cross a plank over a ditch and go through the gate ahead. Ford Whiteadder Water – might be difficult after a rainy spell – and continue along an uphill path to a lane Ⓑ.

Turn left for ½ mile (800m) above the winding Whiteadder Water and, just after first a left- and then a right-hand bend, you reach a ford beyond which is a cattle-grid Ⓒ. Here turn left along a broad track; this is the Herring Road, an ancient routeway across the hills that linked the fishing port of Dunbar with its markets inland. Recross the Whiteadder, this time by a footbridge, go through a gate and continue along the broad, winding, uphill track. The track later straightens out and, where it bends right, continue by a wire fence on the left across the moorland. Go through a gate, keep ahead and, after the fence turns left, continue across rough grass to join and walk along a clear, well-constructed track again.

A few yards after going through a gate to the right of a small group of conifers, the track bears right. Keep straight ahead here across rough grass

and heather to climb a stile by a public footpath sign. Continue in the same direction, following a broad swathe of heather and rough grass through a young conifer plantation to reach a stony track by two public footpath signs. Cross the track, continue along a reasonably discernible path through the young conifers and, soon after descending to cross a small burn, head up a steep embankment to a public footpath sign in front of a metal gate and by a fence corner and broken wall. Go through the gate and continue uphill, by a wire fence on the left, to the fence corner.

Turn left Ⓓ, here leaving the Herring Road, to walk across open moorland along a grassy path by a fence, still bordering a plantation on the left. At the corner of the plantation, go through a gate and keep ahead, still by a wire fence on the left, across the wide-open expanses of Dunbar Common. Go through a metal gate, continue and, after the fence on the left ends, keep straight ahead across moorland. At this point the path is unclear in places, and there is some rough and difficult walking, but keep in a straight line all the while until a discernible path reappears, and later still a clear, grassy track emerges. All the way there are magnificent views across the lowlands to the coast, with both North Berwick Law and Traprain Law standing out prominently.

Eventually the grassy track heads downhill, curving left and descending more steeply to go through a fence gap to the right of a circular sheepfold. Continue downhill, pass to the left of a house to reach a gate, go through and head uphill to Deuchrie Farm. Go through a metal gate, pass between the house and farm buildings and continue along a tarmac drive to reach a lane at a bend. Retrace your steps to the start. ●

Lammer Law and the Hopes Reservoir

Start	Longyester telephone box
Distance	8½ miles (13.7km)
Approximate time	4½ hours
Parking	Off road parking near start and on road to Hopes Reservoir which has wide grassy verges (do not park in gateways or passing places)
Refreshments	None
Ordnance Survey maps	Landranger 66 (Edinburgh, Penicuik & North Berwick) Explorer 345 (Lammermuir Hills, Dalkeith, Bonnyrigg & Gifford)

This route takes the walker to the summit of the Lammermuir Hills which proves to be a magnificent viewpoint. However for most people the highlight of the walk will be the unfrequented walk by Hopes Water which leads to the shoreline of Hopes Reservoir.

Walk south-westwards past Longyester Farm and keep ahead **A** past the dead-end sign. There is pleasant walking on a metalled road which climbs gently to the end of Blinkbonny Wood. The fields by the road are occupied by rams and their families in the summer (there are also cattle). At the end of the metalled road go through a gate bearing a notice that the onward track is a right of way going to Carfraemill **B**. It can be seen ahead wandering up the contours of Threep Law.

The climb proves to be enjoyable and the view looking back improves as height is gained, giving an excuse for breathers. The Hopes Reservoir comes into view as the summit is approached. Go through a gate – the fence is now to the right – and continue to another gate on the right bearing the notice 'No access for mountain bikes' **C**. Go through this gate and walk by the fence to a track. Bear right on to this and then, opposite a gate, turn left to walk to the summit of Lammer Law with its large cairn and triangulation pillar at 1729ft (527m),

Dusk view from Lammer Law

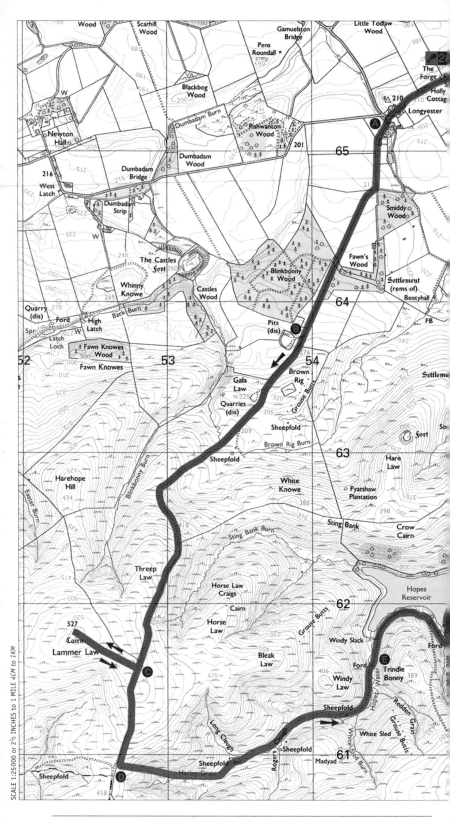

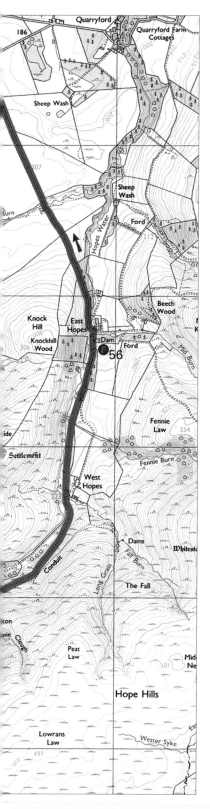

the highest point of the Lammermuir Hills. It will have taken about 90 minutes to reach the summit. The view northwards is extensive and it is said that the Cairngorms may be seen in exceptional conditions. Certainly the main landmarks of the Forth coast and estuary are more readily seen.

Turn back to the right of way and turn right to resume walking southwards. The track descends gently to reach a gate ⬤. Do not go through the gate but turn to the left to descend over heather to pass a line of butts and reach Harley Grain, a mini-ravine which drops steeply at first to pass through a cordon of thistles and nettles which will not be appreciated by anyone wearing shorts. Once this hazard is passed a path becomes discernible to the left of the burn. This soon reaches the head of a beautiful valley where the walking is on smooth greensward. The path crosses the burn several times and gradually becomes a track which fords the burn close to a corrugated sheep enclosure and hut. Further on there are beehives by a similar enclosure.

The track rises above the burn and soon gives a glimpse of the Hopes Reservoir. Look out for herons here. With the reservoir in view the track fords Hopes Water for the last time ⬤ and runs above the man-made lake; the views are splendid.

After the grass-covered dam the track descends to West Hopes giving fine views northwards. The track becomes a surfaced road after a gate at East Hopes which is a popular place for people to leave their cars ⬤. After this the return to Longyester is straightforward walking on about 2 miles (3.2km) of well surfaced road. ⬤

Further Information

 ### The Law and Tradition as they affect Walking in Scotland

Walkers following the routes given in this book should not run into problems, but it is as well to know something about the law as it affects access, and also something of the traditions which can be quite different in Scotland from elsewhere in Britain. Most of this is common sense, observing the country code and having consideration for other people and their activities which, after all, may be their livelihood.

It is often said that there is no law of trespass in Scotland. In fact there is, but the trespass itself is not usually a criminal offence. You can be asked to leave any property, and technically 'reasonable force' may be used to obtain your compliance – though the term is not defined! You can be charged with causing damage due to the trespass, but this would be hard to establish if you were just walking on open, wild, hilly country where, whatever the law, in practice there has been a long tradition of free access for recreational walking – something both the Scottish Landowners' Federation and the Mountaineering Council of Scotland do not want to see changed.

There are certain restrictions. Walkers should obey the country code and seasonal restrictions arising from lambing or stalking. Where there is any likelihood of such restrictions this is mentioned in the text and visitors are asked to comply. When camping, use a campsite. Camp fires should not be lit; they are a danger to moorland and forest, and really not necessary as lightweight and efficient stoves are now available.

Many of the walks in this book are on rights of way. The watchdog on rights of way in Scotland is the Scottish Rights of Way Society (SRWS), who maintain details on all established cases and will, if need be, contest attempted closures. They produce a booklet on the Scottish legal position (Rights of Way, A Guide to the Law in Scotland, 1991), and their green signposts are a familiar sight by many footpaths and tracks, indicating the lines of historic routes.

In Scotland rights of way are not marked on Ordnance Survey maps as is the case south of the border. It was not felt necessary to show these as such on the maps – a further reflection of the freedom to roam that is enjoyed in Scotland. So a path on a map is no indication of a right of way, and many paths and tracks of great use to walkers were built by estates as stalking paths or for private access. While you may traverse such paths, taking due care to avoid damage to property and the natural environment, you should obey restricted access notices and leave if asked to do so.

The only established rights of way are those where a court case has resulted in a legal judgment, but there are thousands of other 'claimed' rights of way. Local planning authorities have a duty to protect rights of way – no easy task with limited resources. Many attempts at closing claimed rights of way have been successfully contested in the courts by the Scottish Rights of Way Society and local authorities.

A dog on a lead or under control may also be taken on a right of way. There is little chance of meeting a free-range solitary bull on any of the walks. Any herds seen are not likely to be dairy cattle, but all cows can be inquisitive and may approach walkers, especially if they have a dog. Dogs running among stock may be shot on the spot; this is not draconian legislation but a desperate attempt to stop sheep and lambs being harmed, driven to panic or lost, sometimes with fatal results. Any practical points or restrictions applicable will be made in the text. If there is no comment it can be assumed that the route carries no real restrictions.

Scotland in fact likes to keep everything

as natural as possible, so, for instance, waymarking is kept to a minimum (the Scottish Rights of Way Society signposts and Forest Walk markers are in unobtrusive colours). In Scotland people are asked to 'walk softly in the wilderness, to take nothing except photographs, and leave nothing except footprints' – which is better than any law.

Scotland's Hills and Mountains: a Concordat on Access

This remarkable agreement was published early in 1996 and is likely to have considerable influence on walkers' rights in Scotland in the future. The signatories include organisations which have formerly been at odds - the Scottish Landowners' Federation and the Ramblers' Association, for example. However they joined with others to make the Access Forum (a full list of signatories is detailed below). The RSPB and the National Trust for Scotland did not sign the Concordat

initially but it is hoped that they will support its principles.

The signatories of the Concordat are:

Association of Deer Management Groups
Convention of Scottish Local Authorities
Mountaineering Council of Scotland
National Farmers' Union of Scotland
Ramblers' Association Scotland
Scottish Countryside Activities Council
Scottish Landowners' Federation
Scottish Natural Heritage
Scottish Sports Association
Scottish Sports Council

They agreed that the basis of access to the hills for the purposes of informal recreation should be:

Freedom of access exercised with responsibility and subject to reasonable constraints for management and conservation purposes.

Acceptance by visitors of the needs of land management, and understanding of

Further Information

Threipmuir Reservoir, Balerno

how this sustains the livelihood, culture and community interests of those who live and work in the hills.

Acceptance by land managers of the public's expectation of having access to the hills.

Acknowledgment of a common interest in the natural beauty and special qualities of Scotland's hills, and the need to work together for their protection and enhancement.

The Forum point out that the success of the Concordat will depend on all who

---

 ## Glossary of Gaelic Names

Many of the place-names in Scotland are Gaelic in origin, and this list gives some of the more common elements, which will allow readers to understand otherwise meaningless words and appreciate the relationship between place-names and landscape features. Place-names often have variant spellings, and the more common of these are given here.

aber	mouth of loch, river	eilidh	hind
abhainn	river	eòin, eun	bird
allt	stream	fionn	white
auch, ach	field	fraoch	heather
bal, bail, baile	town, homestead	gabhar, ghabhar,	
bàn	white, fair, pale	gobhar	goat
bealach	hill pass	garbh	rough
beg, beag	small	geal	white
ben, beinn	hill	ghlas, glas	grey
bhuidhe	yellow	gleann, glen	narrow, valley
blar	plain	gorm	blue, green
brae, braigh	upper slope, steepening	inbhir, inver	confluence
		inch, inis, innis	island, meadow by river
breac	speckled		
cairn	pile of stones, often marking a summit	lag, laggan	hollow
		làrach	old site
cam	crooked	làirig	pass
càrn	cairn, cairn-shaped hill	leac	slab
		liath	grey
caol, kyle	strait	loch	lake
ceann, ken, kin	head	lochan	small loch
cil, kil	church, cell	màm	pass, rise
clach	stone	maol	bald-shaped top
clachan	small village	monadh	upland, moor
cnoc	hill, knoll, knock	mór, mor(e)	big
coille, killie	wood	odhar, odhair	dun-coloured
corrie, coire, choire	mountain hollow	rhu, rubha	point
		ruadh	red, brown
craig, creag	cliff, crag	sgòr, sgòrr,	
crannog, crannag	man-made island	sgùrr	pointed
		sron	nose
dàl, dail	field, flat	stob	pointed
damh	stag	strath	valley (broader than glen)
dearg	red		
druim, drum	long ridge	tarsuinn	traverse, across
dubh, dhu	black, dark	tom	hillock (rounded)
dùn	hill fort	tòrr	hillock (more rugged)
eas	waterfall	tulloch, tulach	knoll
eilean	island	uisge	water, river

manage or visit the hills acting on these four principles. In addition, the parties to the Concordat will promote good practice in the form of:

- Courtesy and consideration at a personal level.
- A welcome to visitors.
- Making advice readily available on the ground or in advance.
- Better information about the uplands and hill land uses through education.
- Respect by visitors for the welfare needs of livestock and wildlife.
- Adherence to relevant codes and standards of good practice by visitors and land managers alike.

Any local restrictions on access should be essential for the needs of management, should be fully explained, and be for the minimum period and area required.

Queries should be addressed to:
Access Forum Secretariat, c/o Recreation and Access Branch,
Scottish Natural Heritage, 2 Anderson Place, Edinburgh EH6 5NP.

Salisbury Crags, Holyrood Park, Edinburgh

 ## Safety on the Hills

The hills and lower but remote areas call for care and respect. The idyllic landscape of the tourist brochures can change rapidly into a world of gales, rain and mist, potentially lethal for those ill-equipped or lacking navigational skills. The Scottish hills in winter can be arctic in severity, and even in summer, snow can lash the summits.

At the very least carry adequate wind- and waterproof outer garments, food and drink to spare, a basic first-aid kit, whistle, map and compass – and know how to use them. Wear boots. Plan within your capabilities. If going alone ensure you leave details of your proposed route. Heed local advice, listen to weather forecasts, and do not hesitate to modify plans if conditions deteriorate.

Some of the walks in this book venture into remote country and others climb high summits, and these expeditions should only be undertaken in good summer conditions. In winter they could well need the skills and experience of mountaineering rather than walking. In midwinter the hours of daylight are of course much curtailed, but given crisp, clear late-winter days many of the shorter expeditions would be perfectly feasible, if the guidelines given are adhered to.

Further Information

Mountain Rescue

In case of emergency the standard procedure is to dial 999 and ask for the police who will assess and deal with the situation.

First, however, render first aid as required and make sure the casualty is made warm and comfortable. The distress signal (six flashes/whistle-blasts, repeated at minute intervals) may bring help from other walkers in the area. Write down essential details: exact location (six-figure reference), time of accident, numbers involved, details of injuries, steps already taken; then despatch a messenger to phone the police.

If leaving the casualty alone, mark the site with an eye-catching object. Be patient; waiting for help can seem interminable.

Useful Organisations

Association for the Protection of Rural Scotland
Gladstone's Land, 3rd floor,
483 Lawnmarket, Edinburgh EH1 2NT
Tel. 0131 225 7012

Forestry Commission
Information Department,
231 Corstorphine Road, Edinburgh
EH12 7AT
Tel. 0131 334 0303

Historic Scotland
Longmore House, Salisbury Place,
Edinburgh EH9 1SH
Tel. 0131 668 8600

Long Distance Walkers' Association
21 Upcroft, Windsor, Berkshire SL4 3NH
Tel. 01753 866685

National Trust for Scotland
5 Charlotte Square, Edinburgh EH2 4DU
Tel. 0131 226 5922

Ordnance Survey
Romsey Road, Southampton SO16 4GU
Tel. 08456 05 05 05 (Lo-call)

Ramblers' Association (main office)
2nd Floor, Camelford House, 87–90 Albert
Embankment, London SE1 7TW
Tel. 020 7339 8500

Ramblers' Association (Scotland)
Kingfisher House, Auld Mart Business
Park, Milnathort, Kinross KY13 9DA
Tel. 01577 861222

Royal Society for the Protection of Birds
Abernethy Forest Reserve, Forest Lodge,
Nethybridge, Inverness-shire PH25 3EF
Tel. 01479 821409

Scottish Landowners' Federation
25 Maritime Street, Edinburgh EH6 5PW
Tel. 0131 555 1031

Scottish Natural Heritage
12 Hope Terrace, Edinburgh EH9 2AS
Tel. 0131447 4784

Scottish Rights of Way Society Ltd
John Cotton Business Centre,
10 Sunnyside, Edinburgh EH7 5RA
Tel. 0131 652 2937

Scottish Wildlife Trust
Cramond House, Kirk Cramond, Cramond
Glebe Road, Edinburgh EH4 6NS
Tel. 0131 312 7765

Scottish Youth Hostels Association
7 Glebe Crescent, Stirling FK8 2JA
Tel. 01786 891400

Tourist Information
Scottish Tourist Board
23 Ravelston Terrace, Edinburgh EH43EU
Tel. 0131 332 2433

Edinburgh & Lothians Tourist Board
4 Rothesay Terrace, Edinburgh EH3 7RY
Tel. 0131 473 3800

Local tourist information offices:
Dunbar: 01368 863353
North Berwick 01620 892197

Weather Forecasts
Scotland two-day forecast
Tel. 0870 510876
UK seven-day forecast
Tel 0891 333123

Ordnance Survey Maps of Edinburgh and Lothians

The area of this title is covered by Ordnance Survey 1:50 000 scale (1$^1/_4$ inches to 1 mile or 2 cm to 1km) Landranger map sheets 65, 66, 67. These all-purpose maps are packed with information to help you explore the area and show viewpoints, picnic sites, places of interest and caravan and camping sites.

To examine the area in more detail and especially if you are planning walks, Ordnance Survey Outdoor Leisure maps 16 and 44 at 1:25 000 (2$^1/_2$ inches to 1 mile or 4cm to 1km) scale are ideal:

The following Explorer maps also at 1:25,000 scale cover the area:

323	324	330
336	339	344
345	349	350
351		

To get to this area use the Ordnance Survey Great Britain Routeplanner Map (Travelmaster map 1) at 1:625 000 (1 inch to 10 miles or 1cm to 6.25 km) scale or Travelmaster map 3 (Southern Scotland and Northumberland) at 1:250 000 (1 inch to 4 miles or 1cm to 2.5km) scale.

Ordnance Survey maps and guides are available from most booksellers, stationers and newsagents.

Further Information

The Forth Road Bridge

Index